I0502542

These designs are made of elements of music. If you look closely at the front of an amp, you can see the interesting pattern of the mesh. You can see the metal wire woven into flowing patterns making up the design of a microphone. Shapes are straight like guitar strings or piano keys. Curves are rounded on drum heads or gracefully shaped in the body of the guitar. Combined together they make beautiful art.

The combinations can be endlessly re-created, or given a different feel with various color changes.

This is volume one of the series.

artrock_designs@yahoo.com

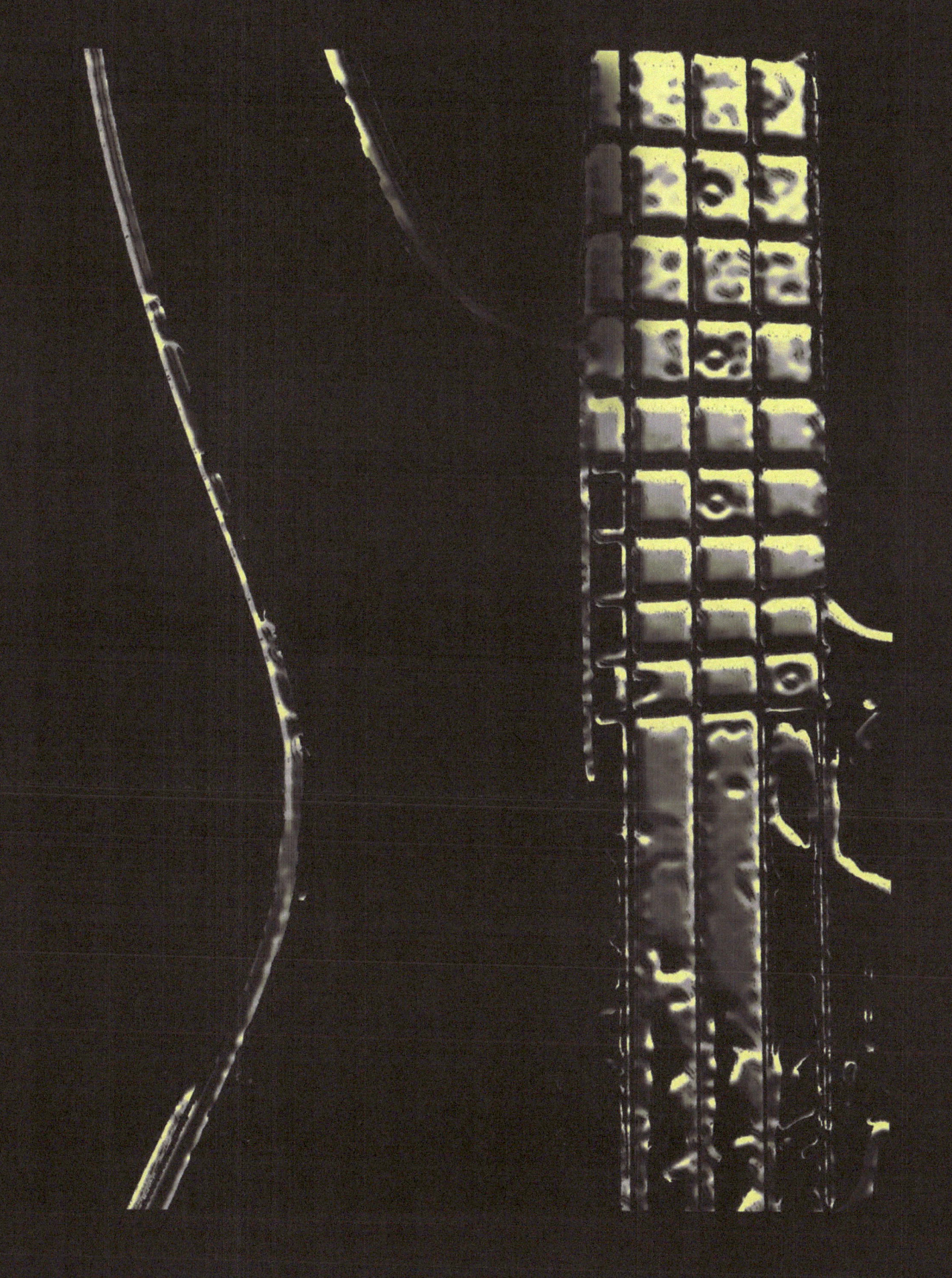

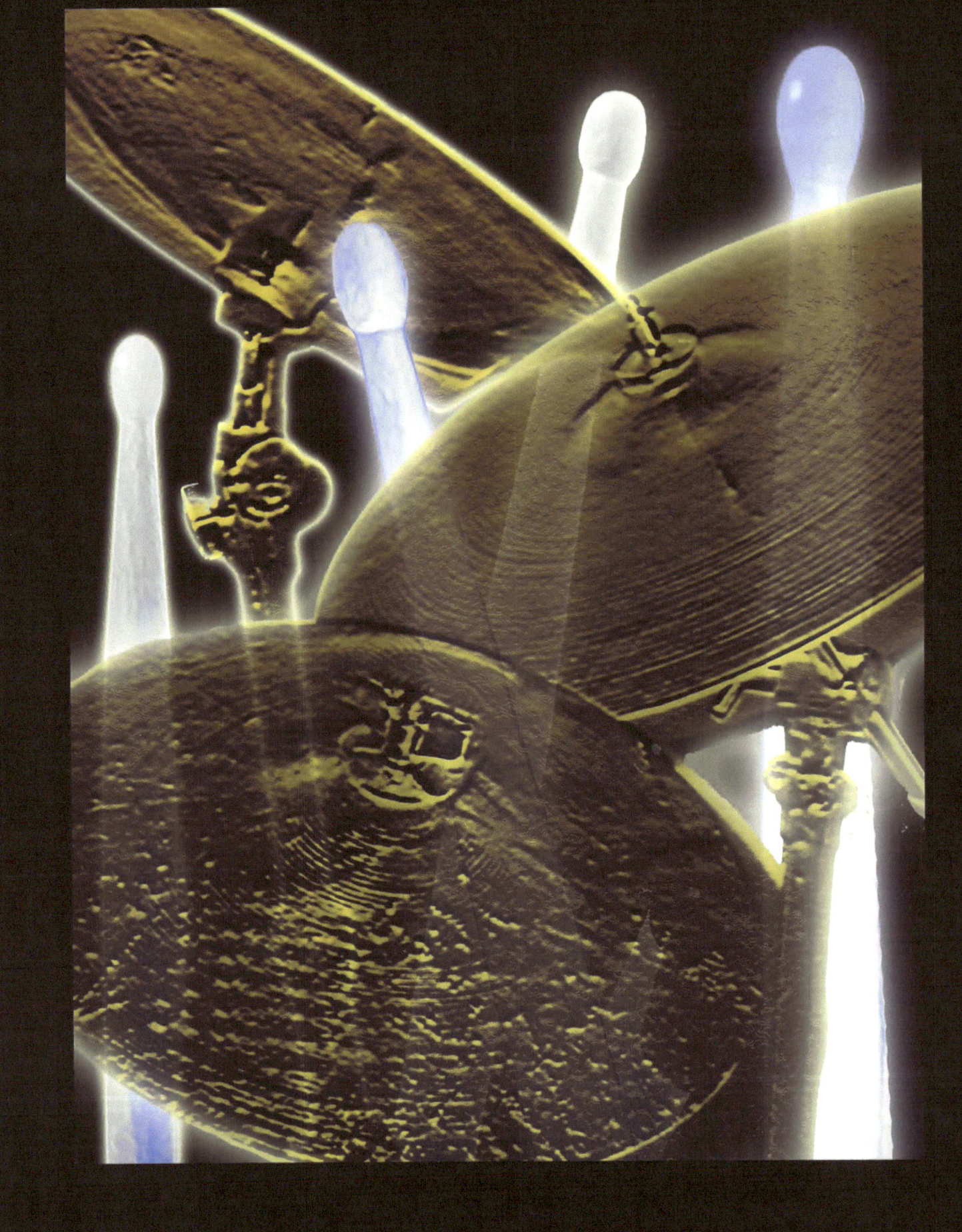

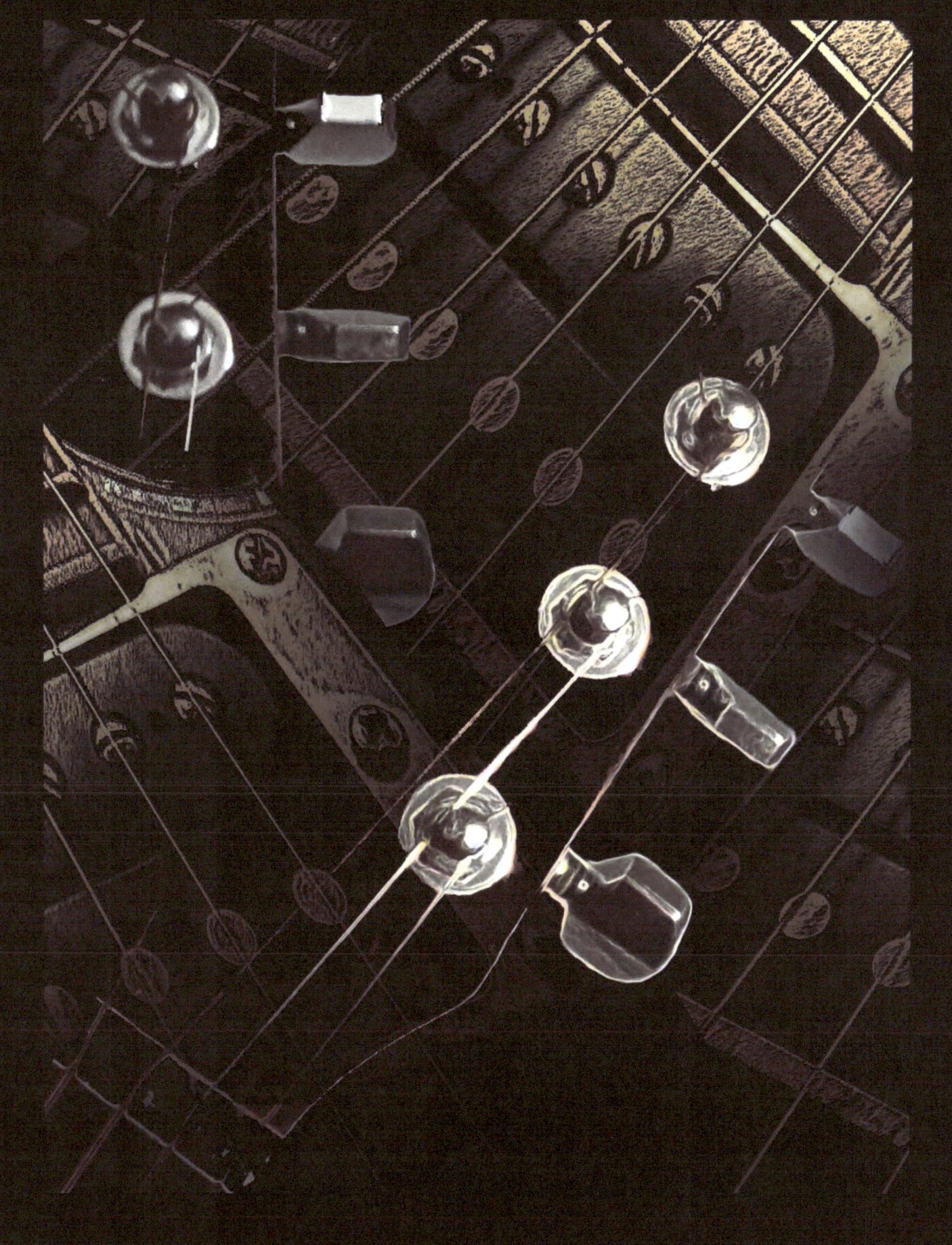

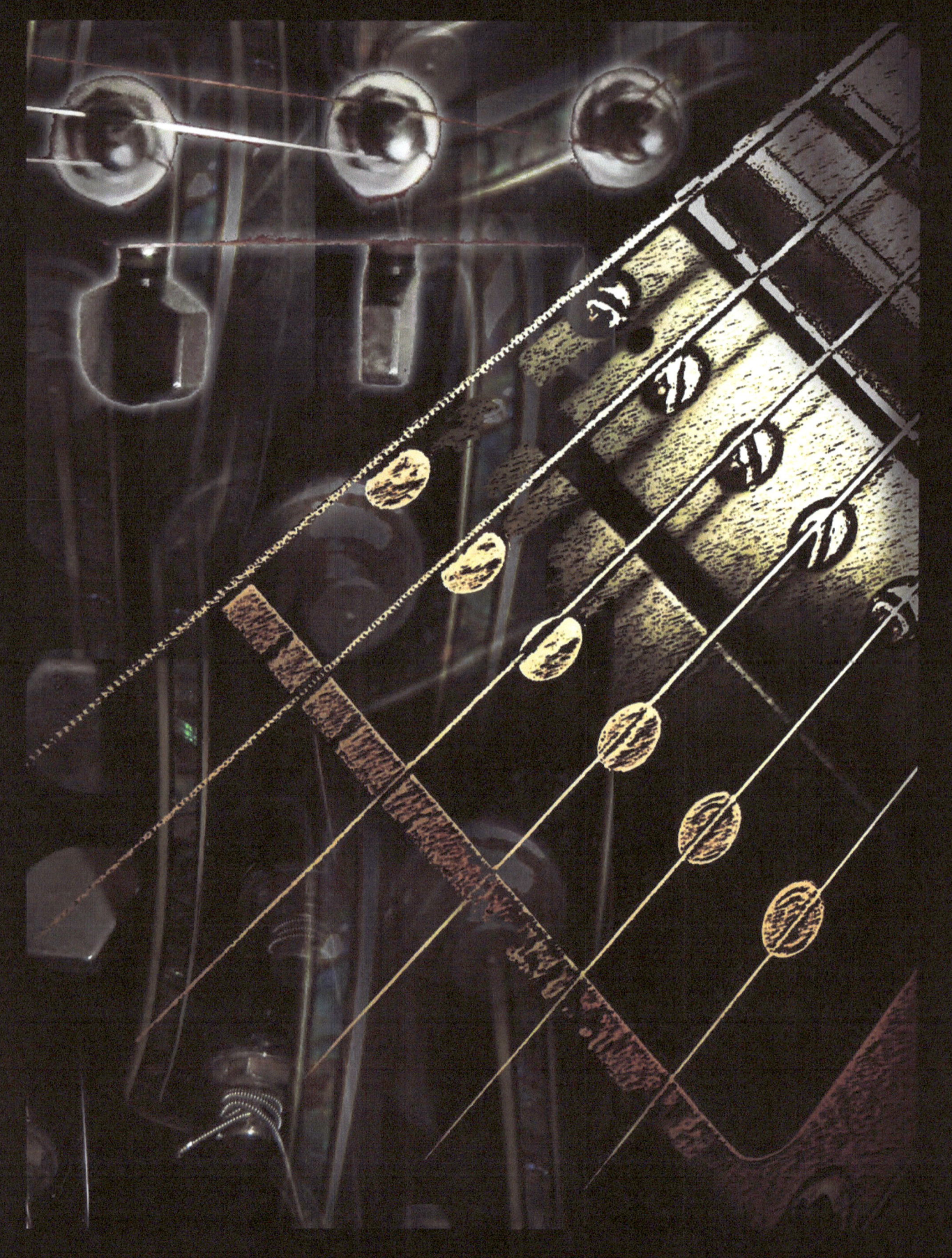

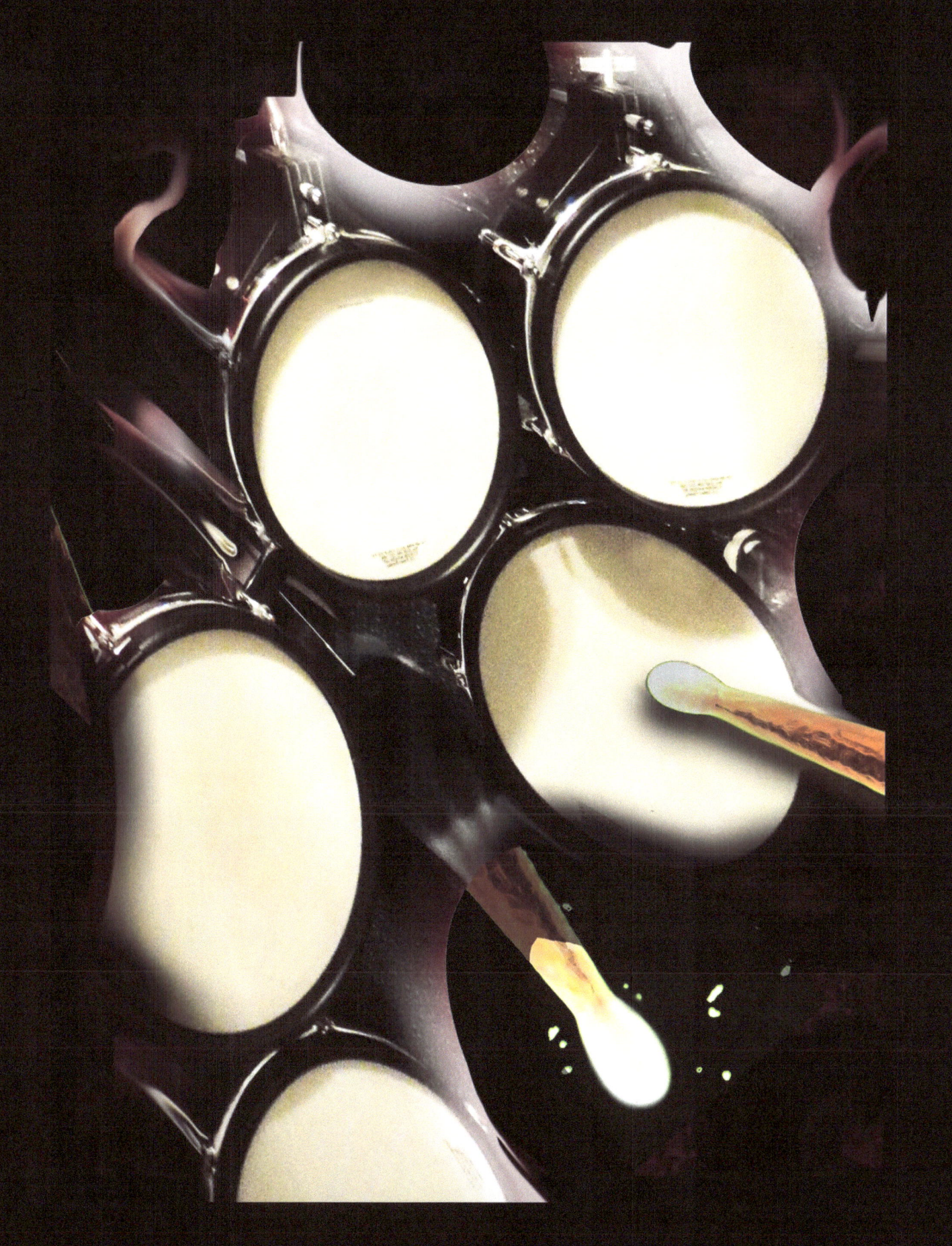

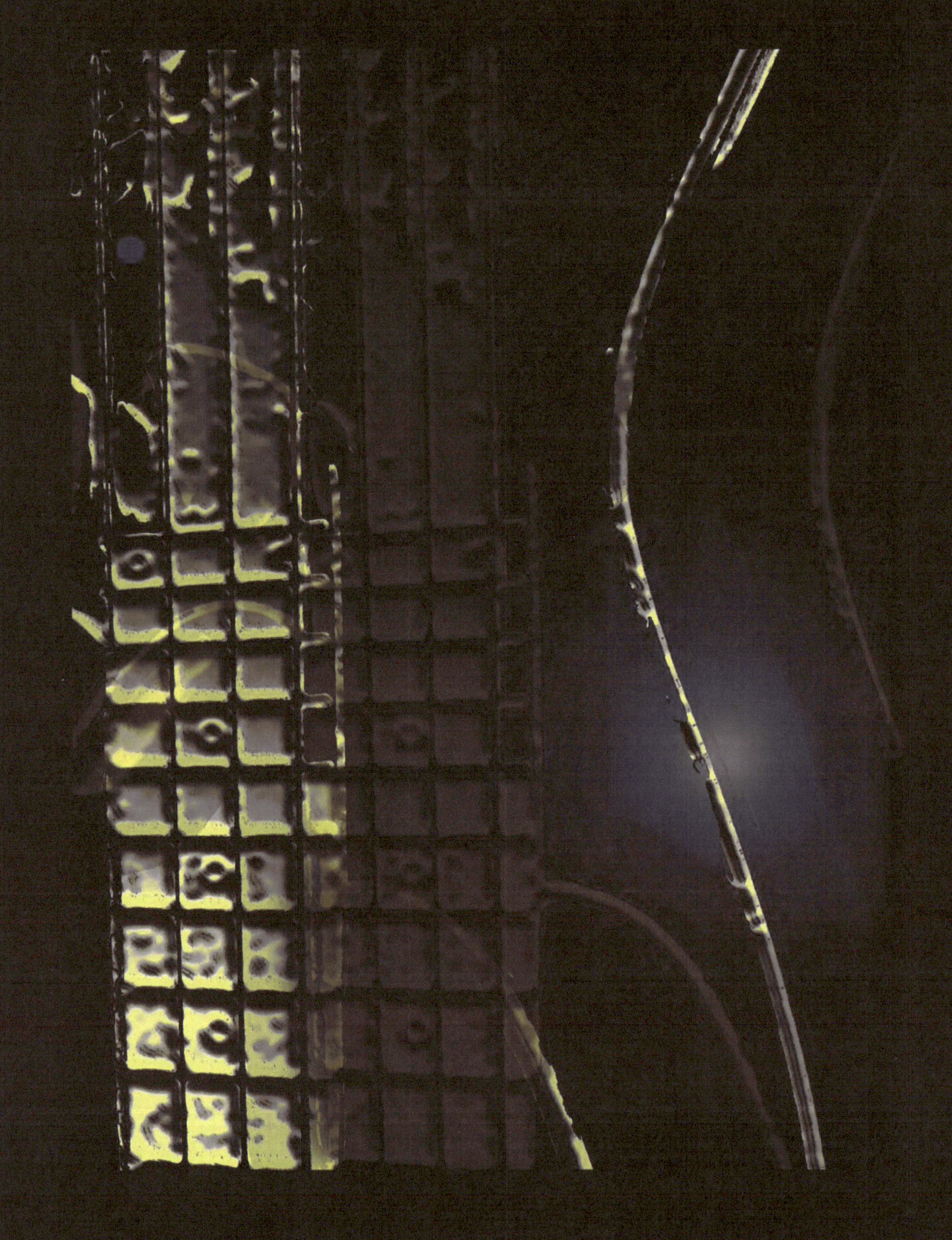

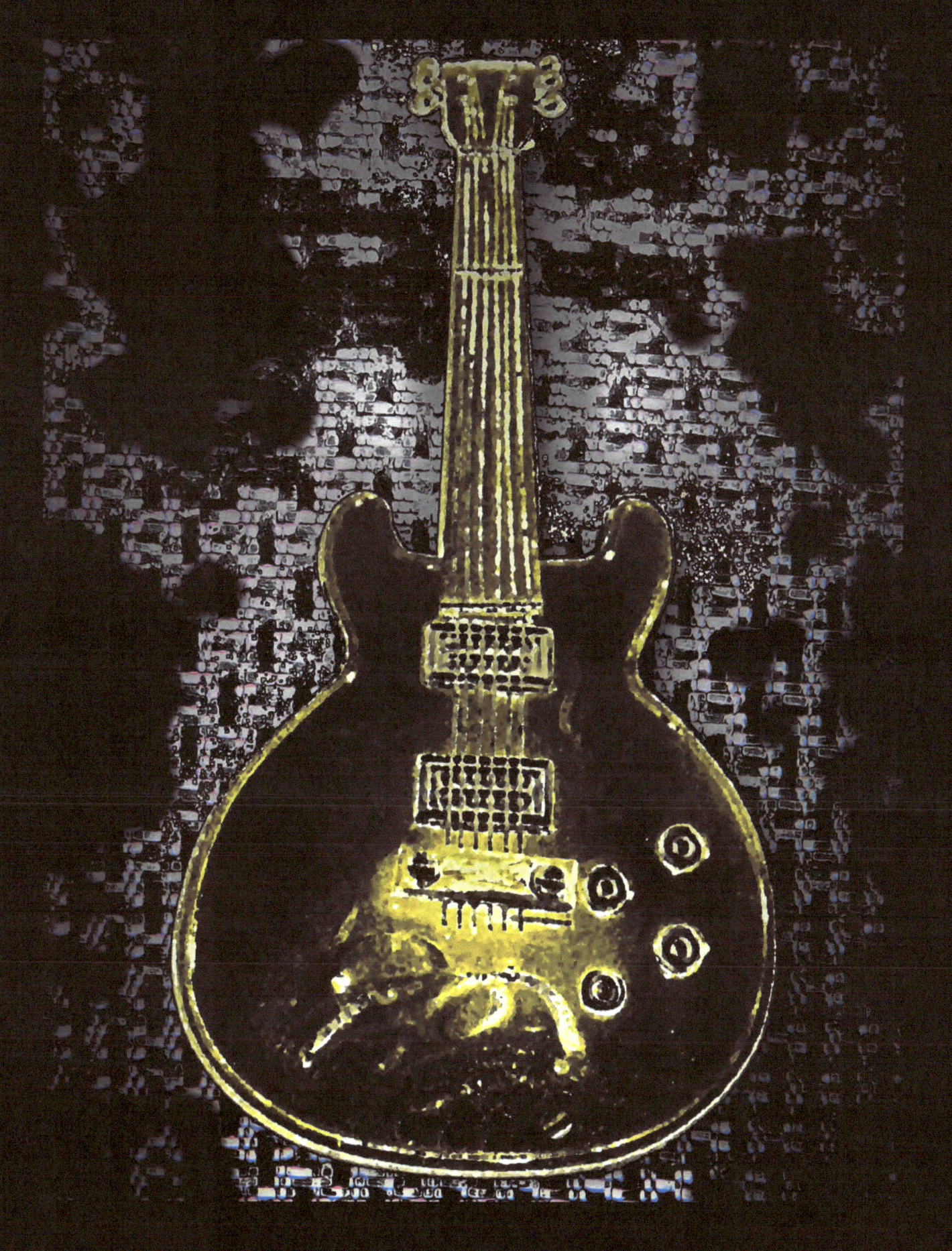

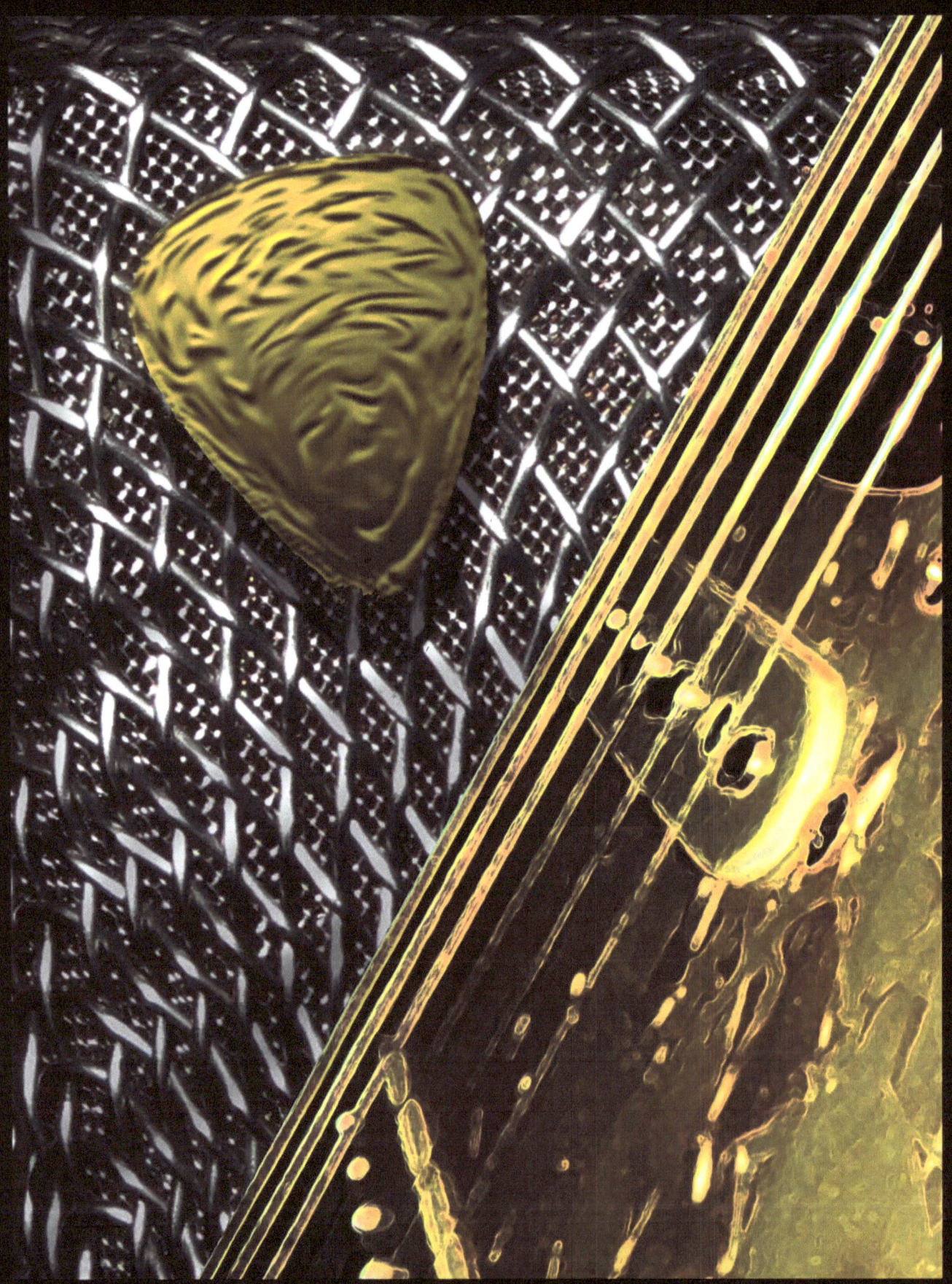

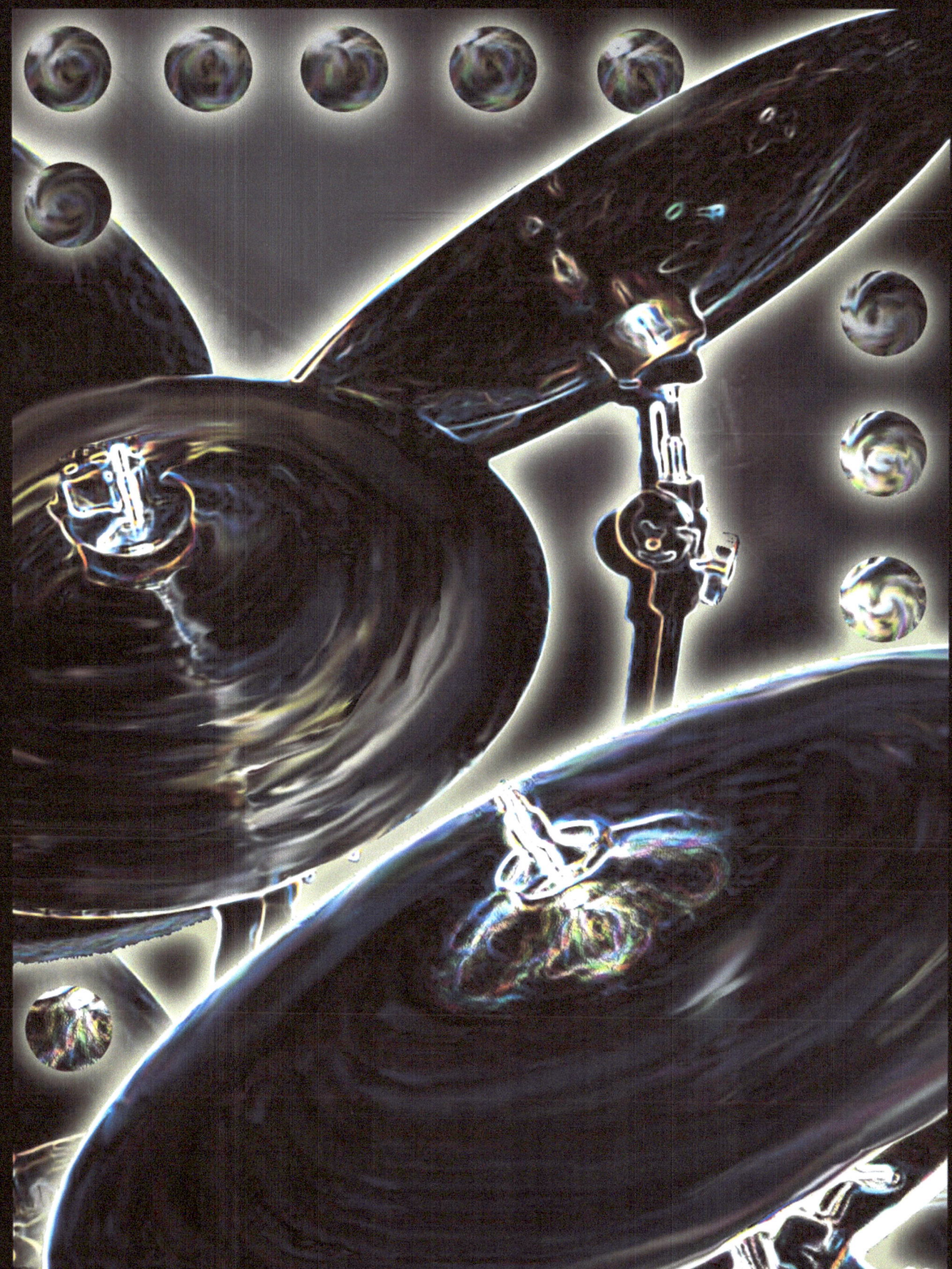

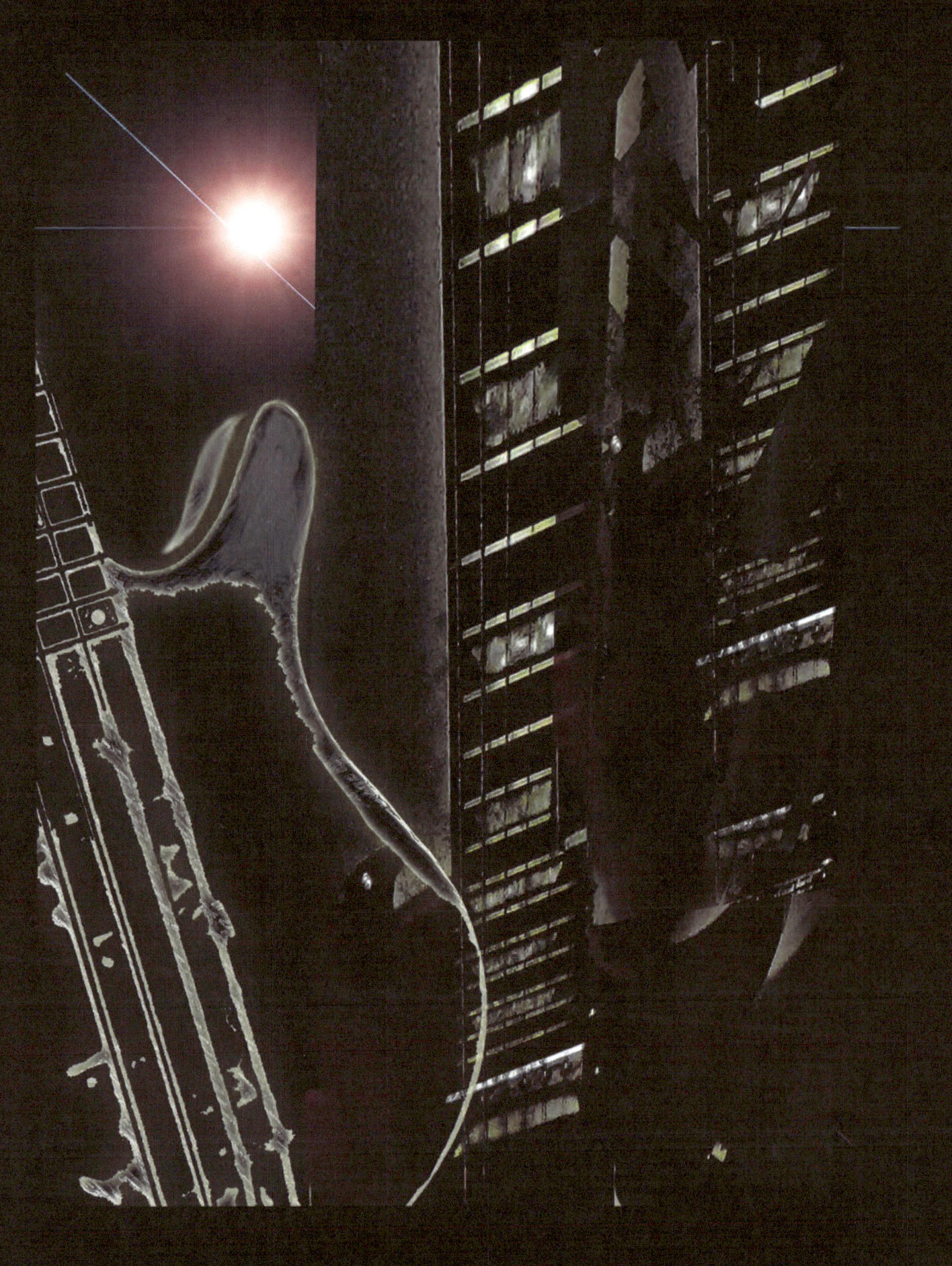

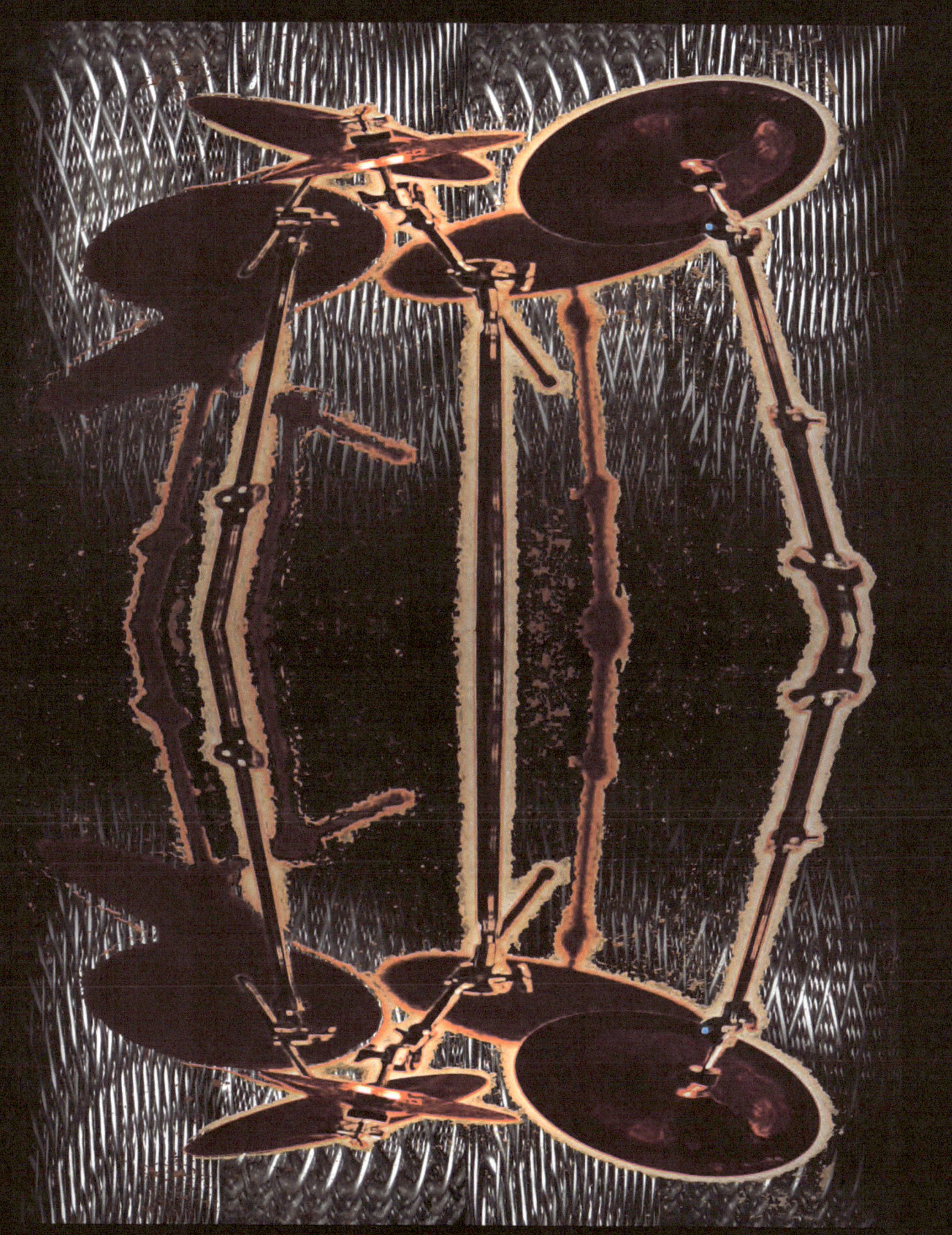

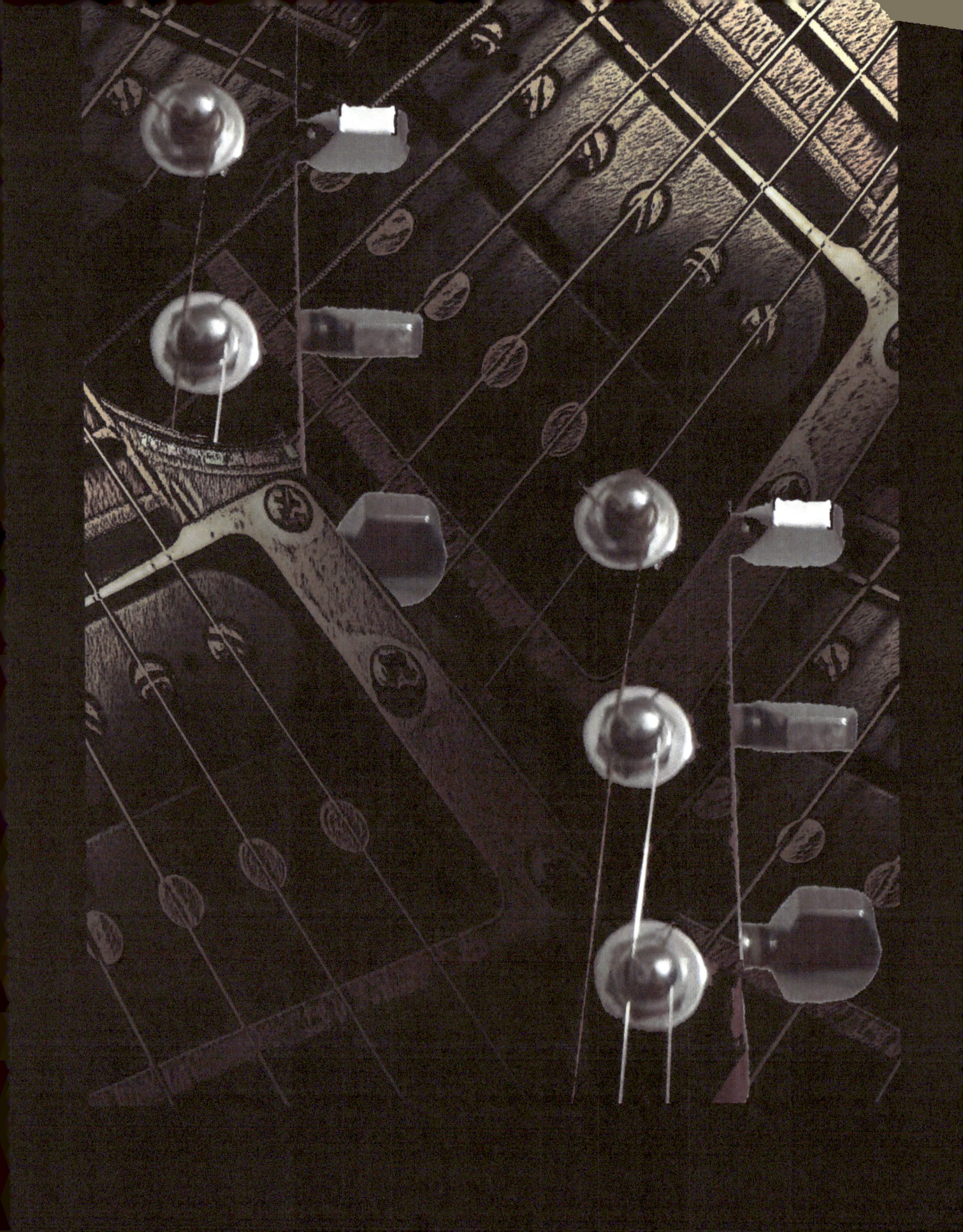

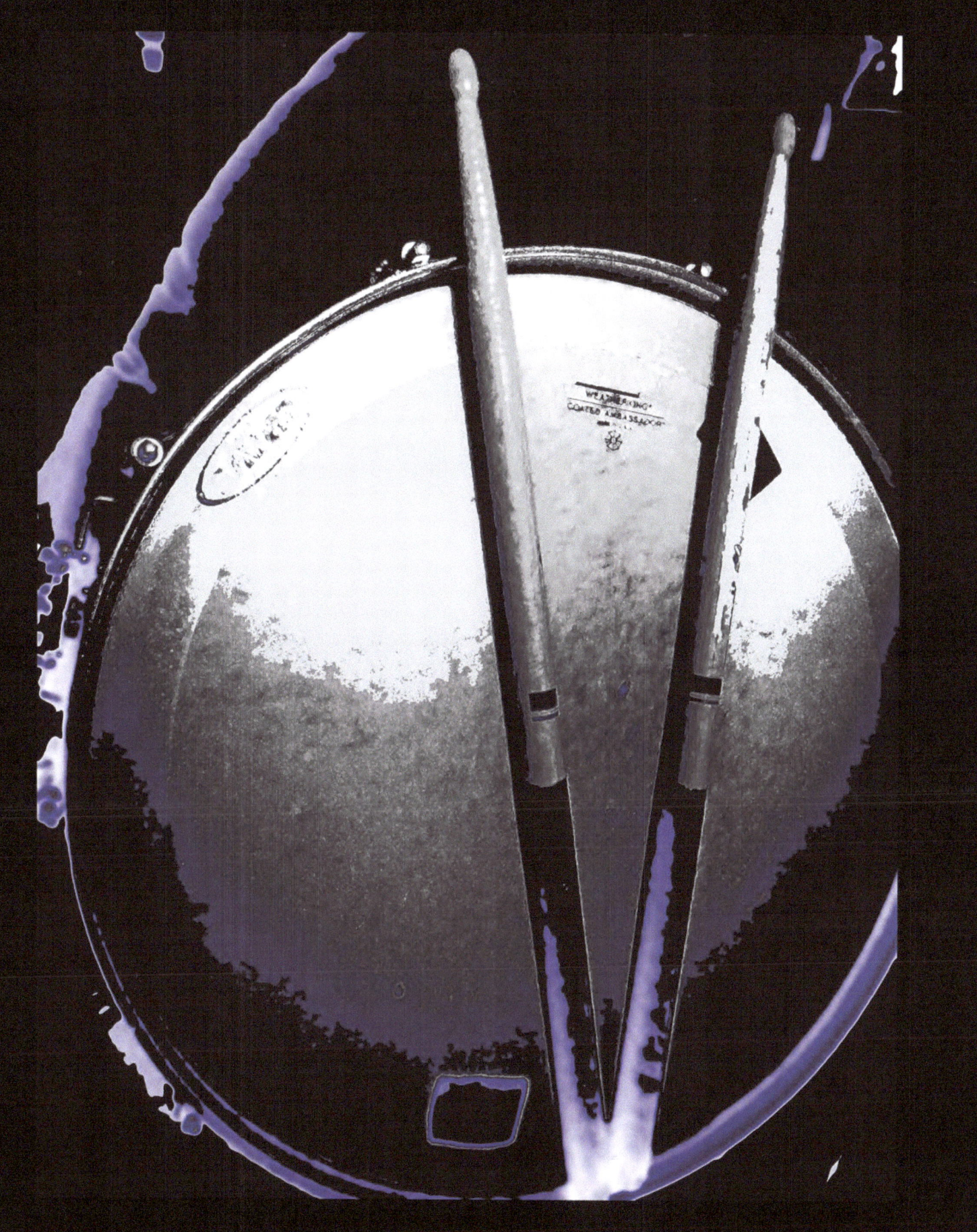

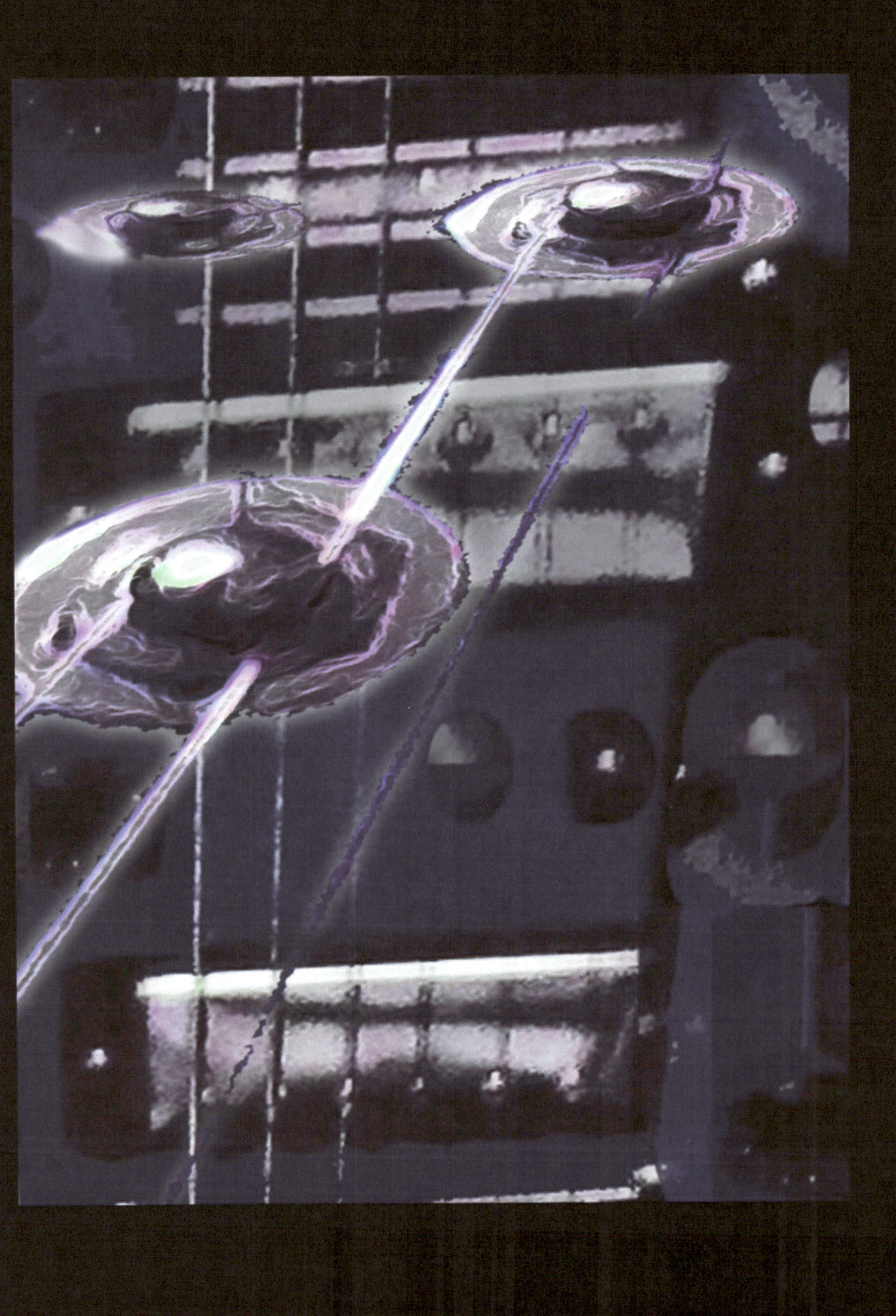

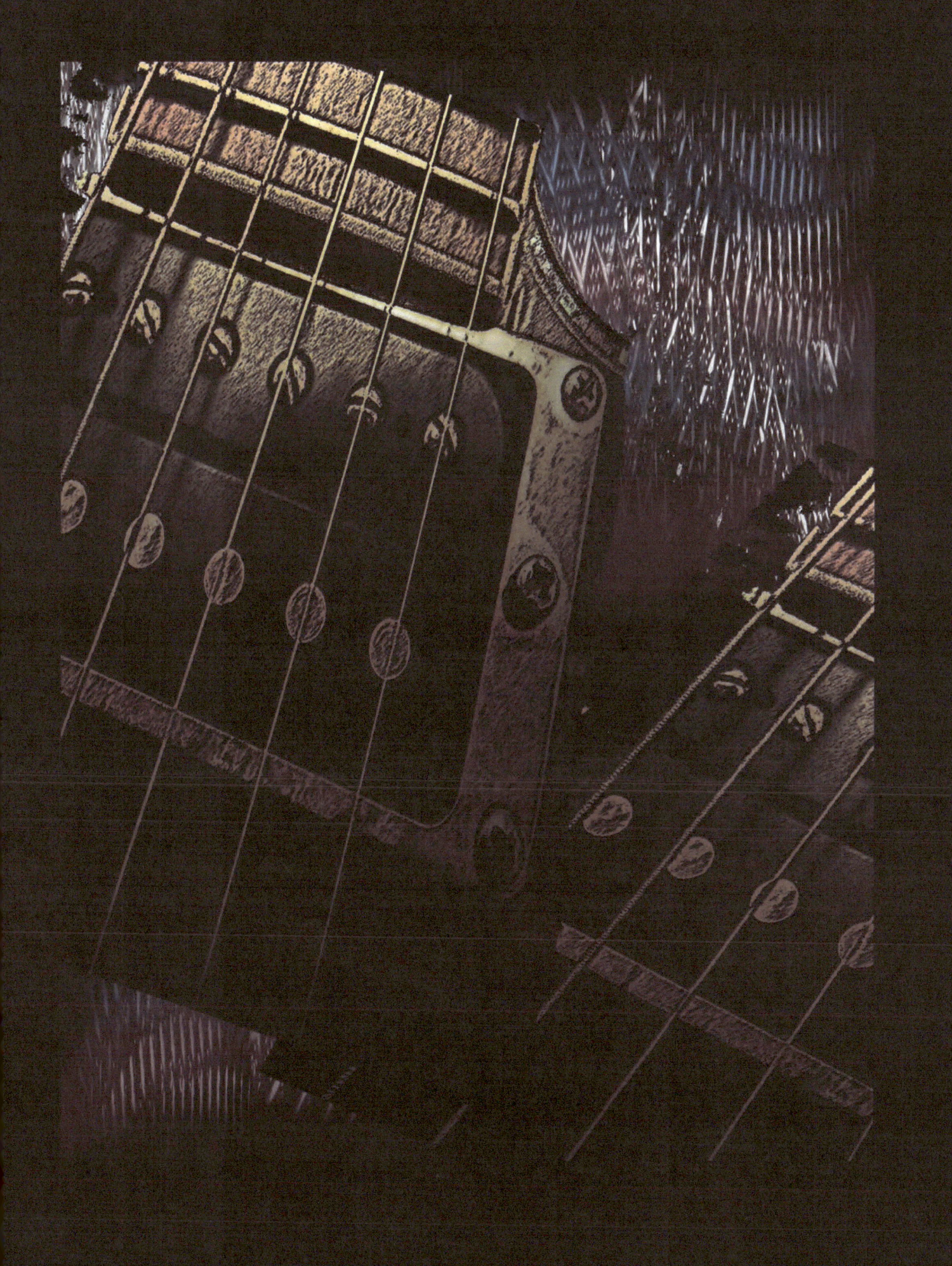

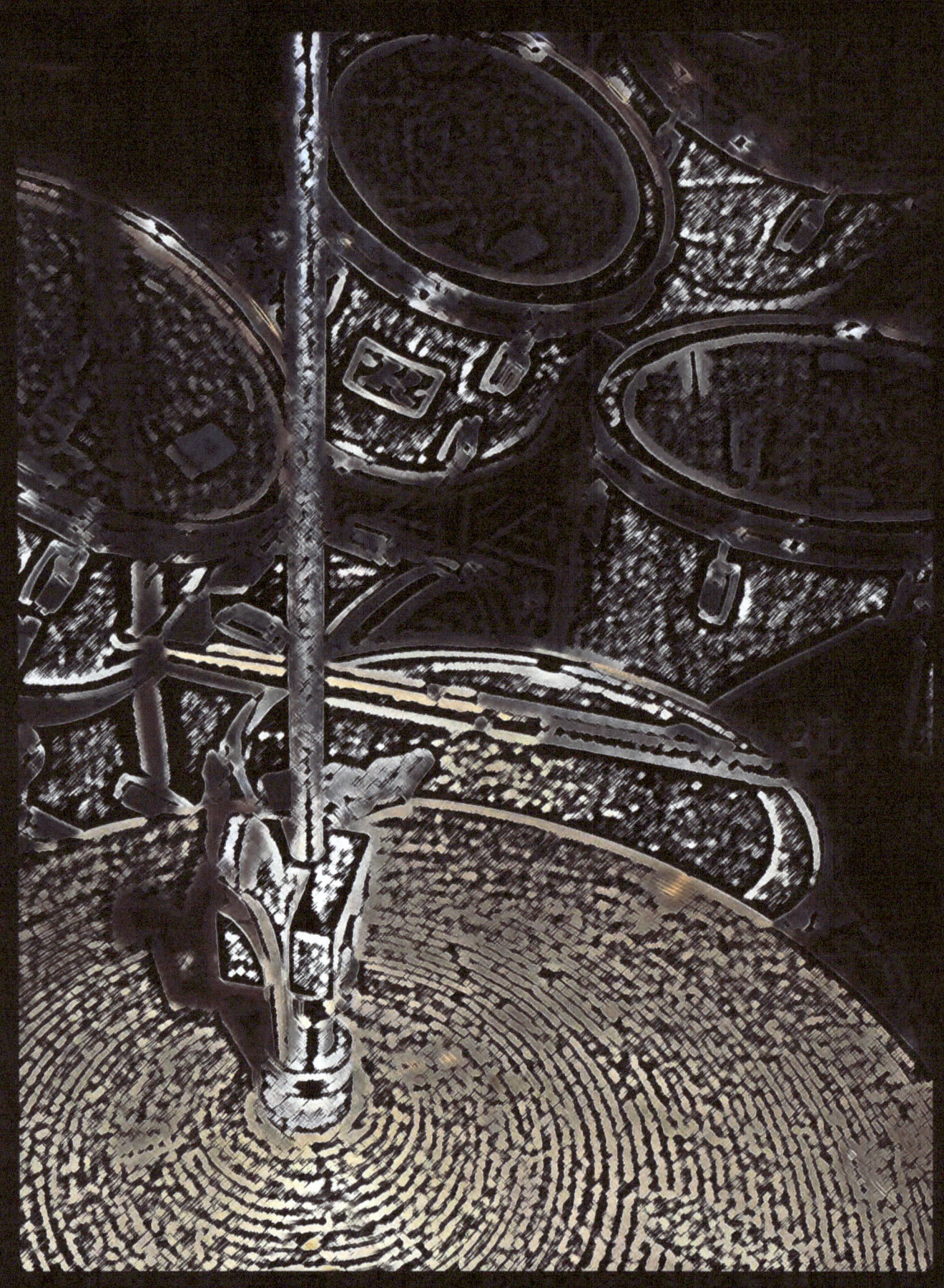

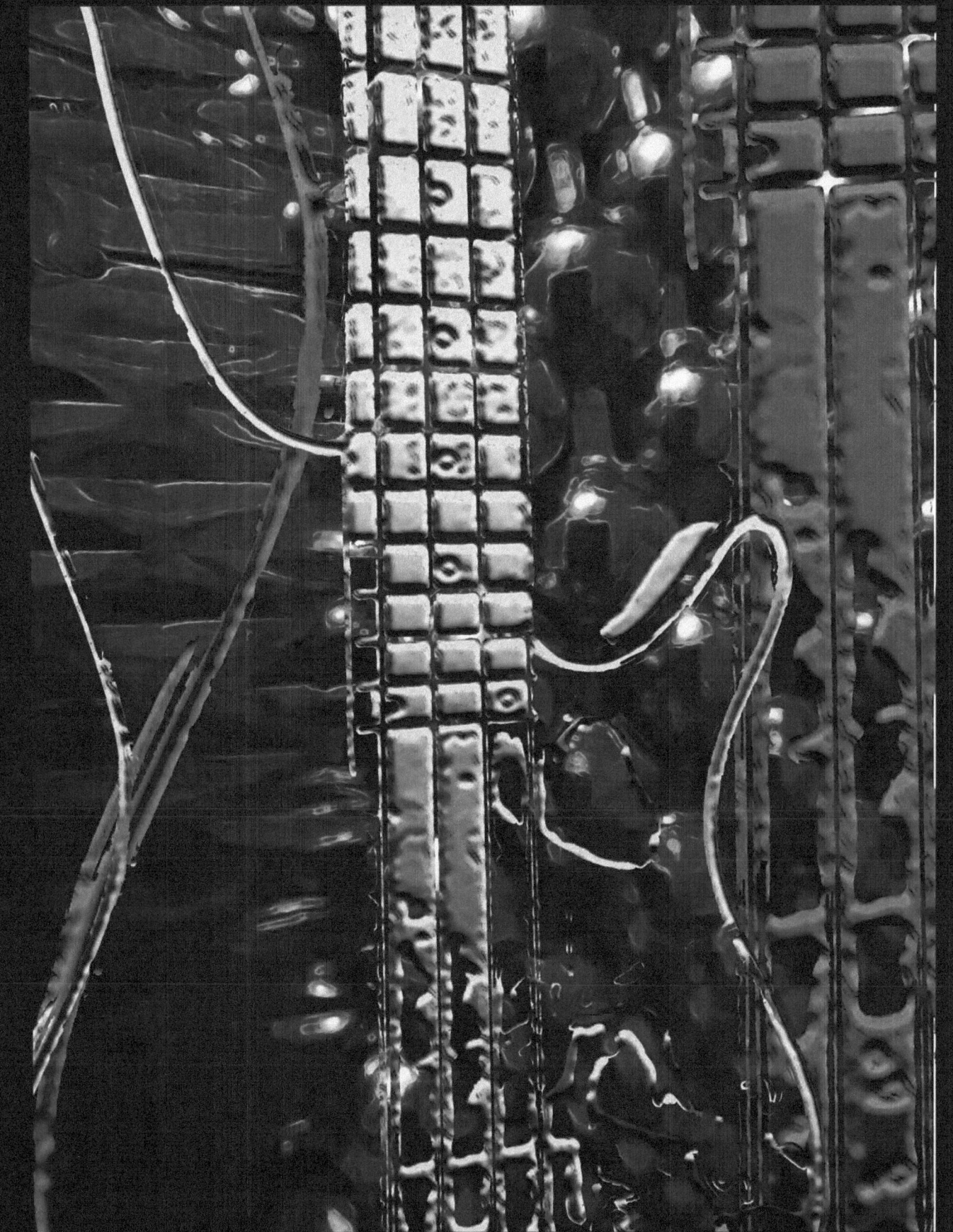

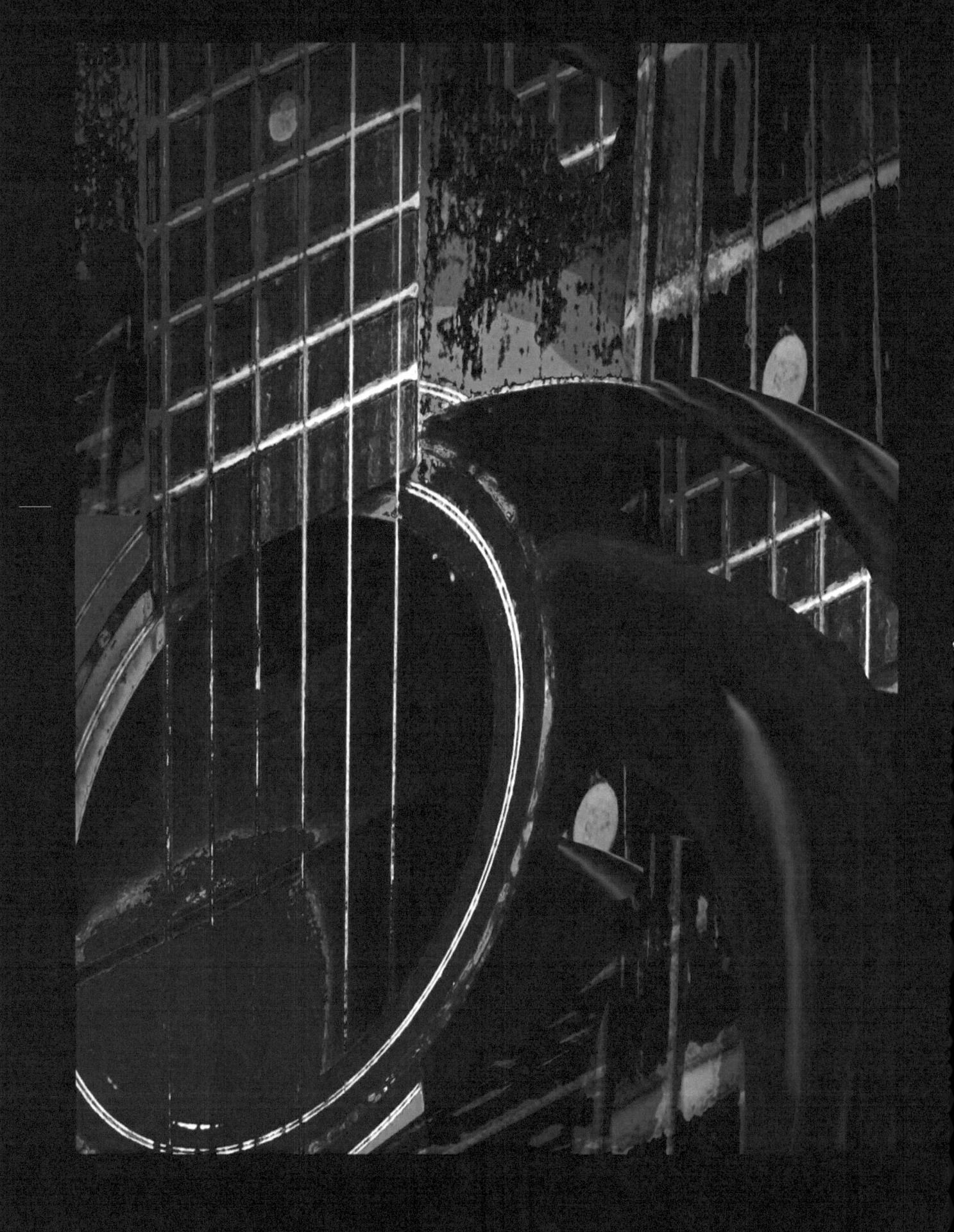

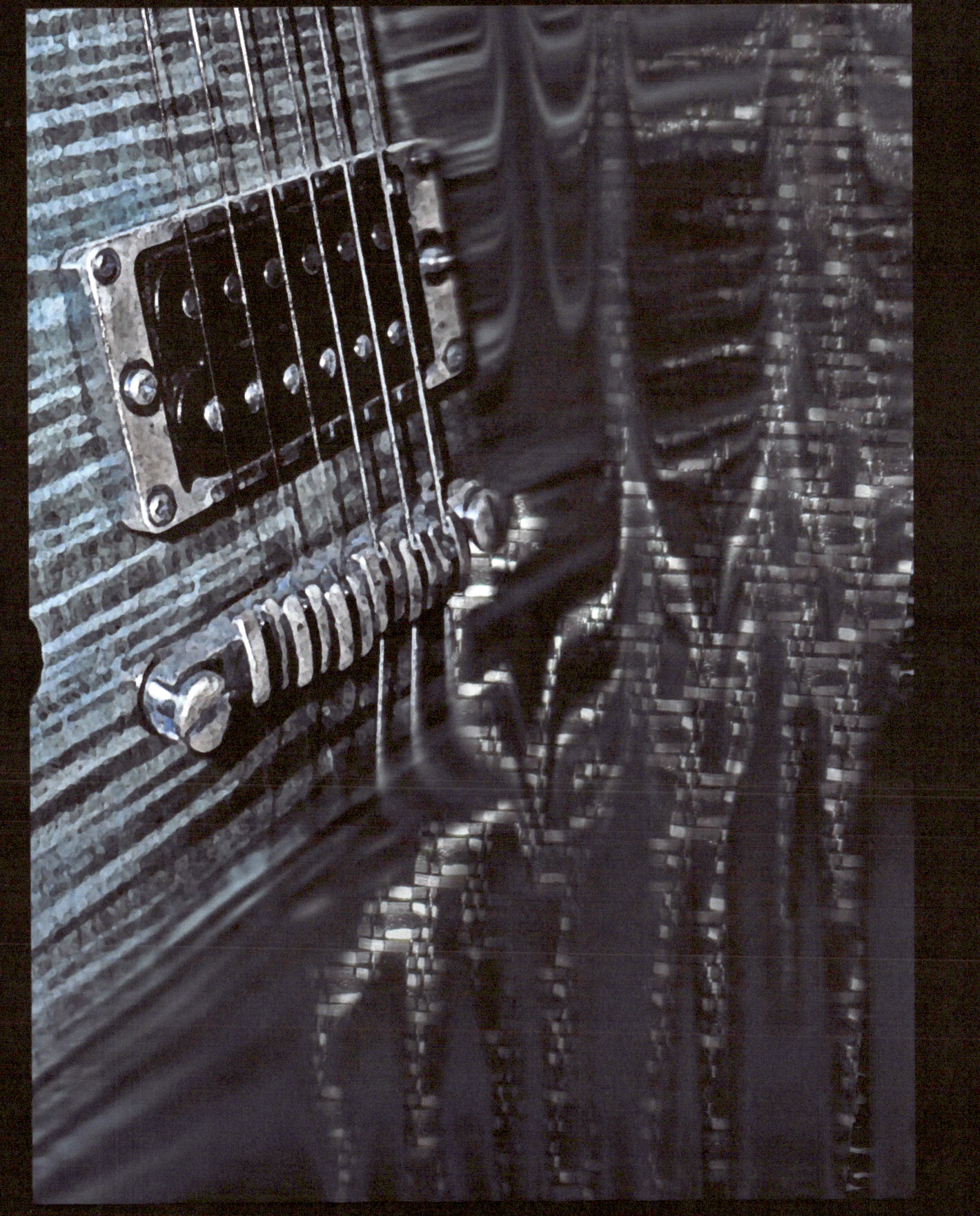

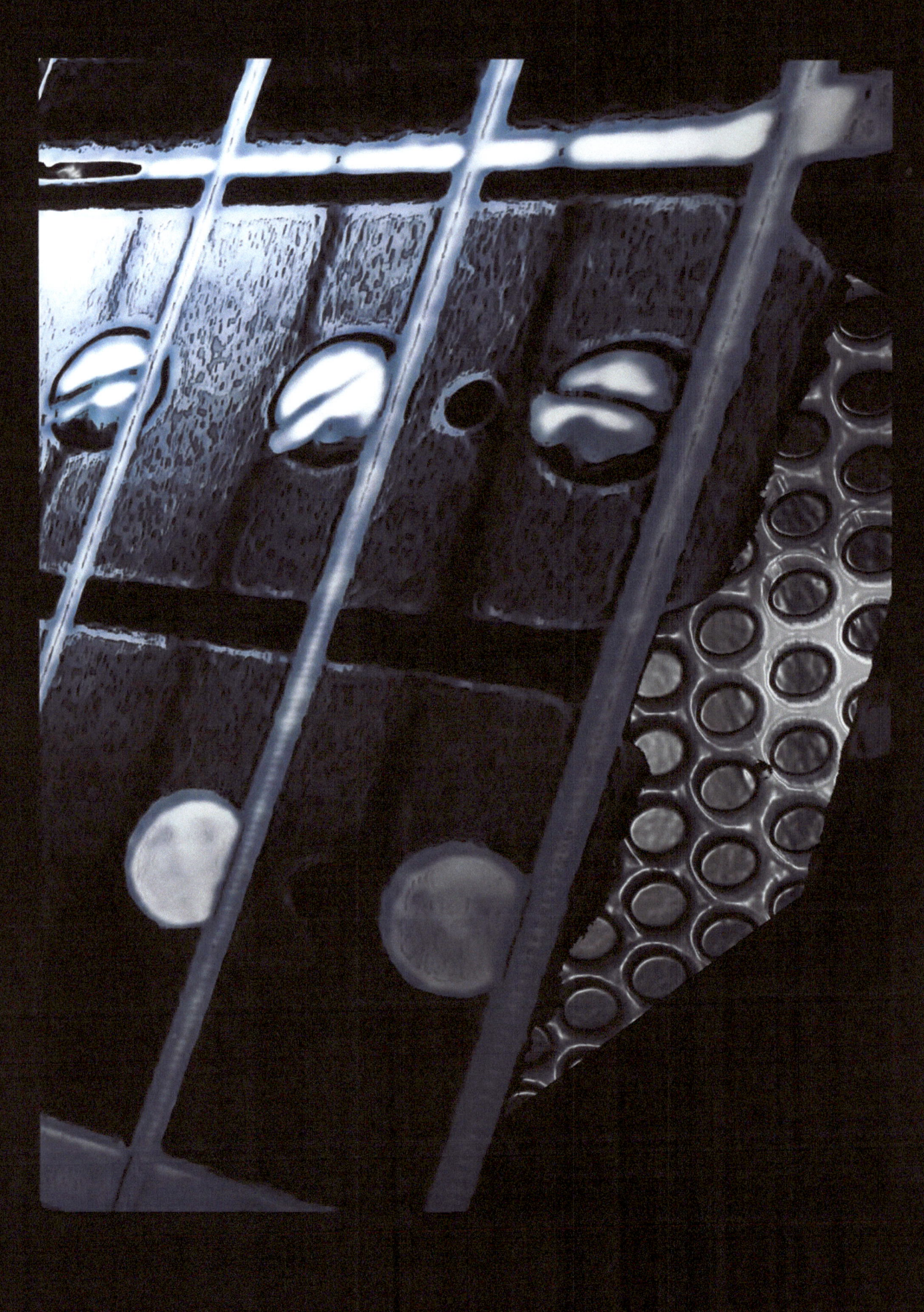

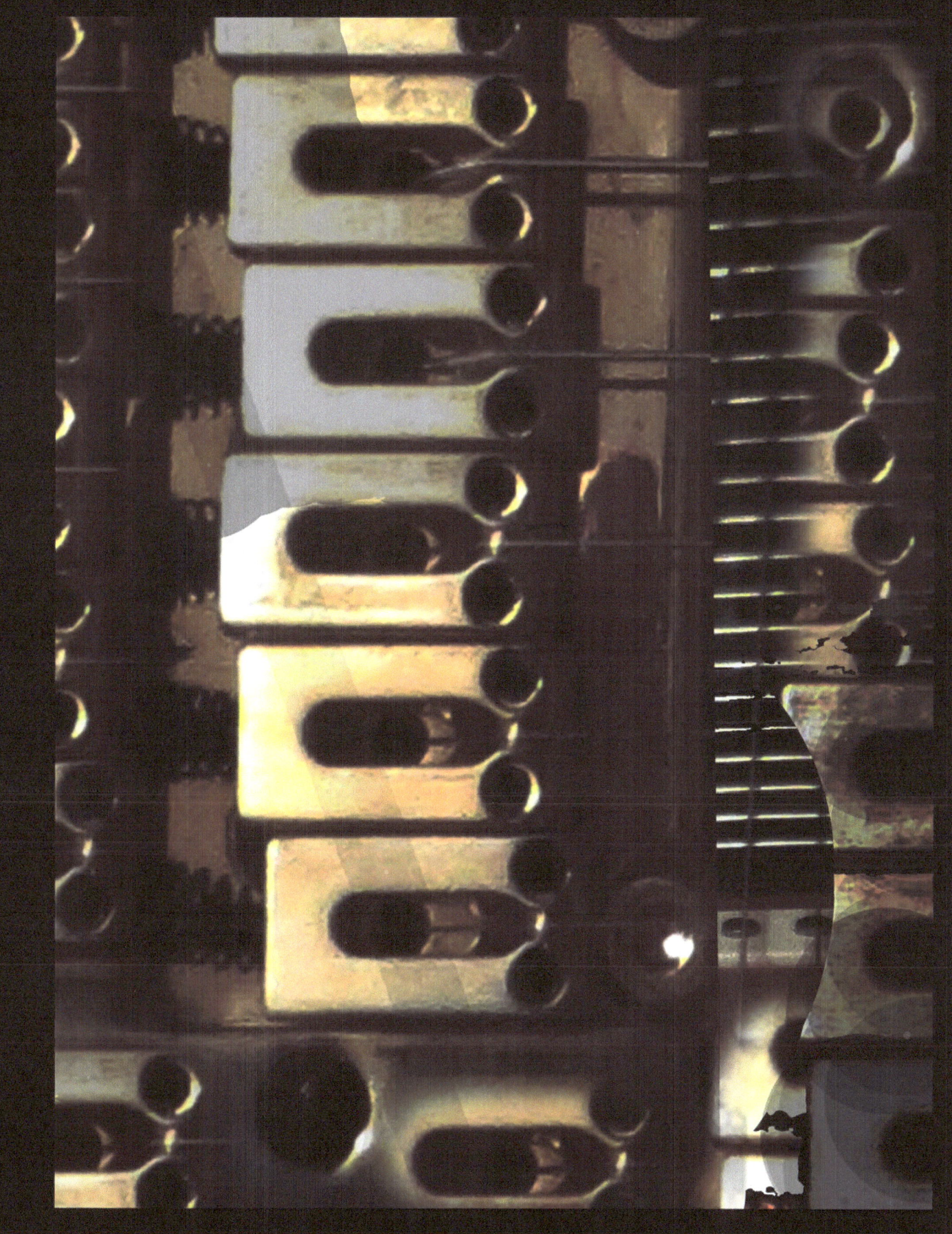

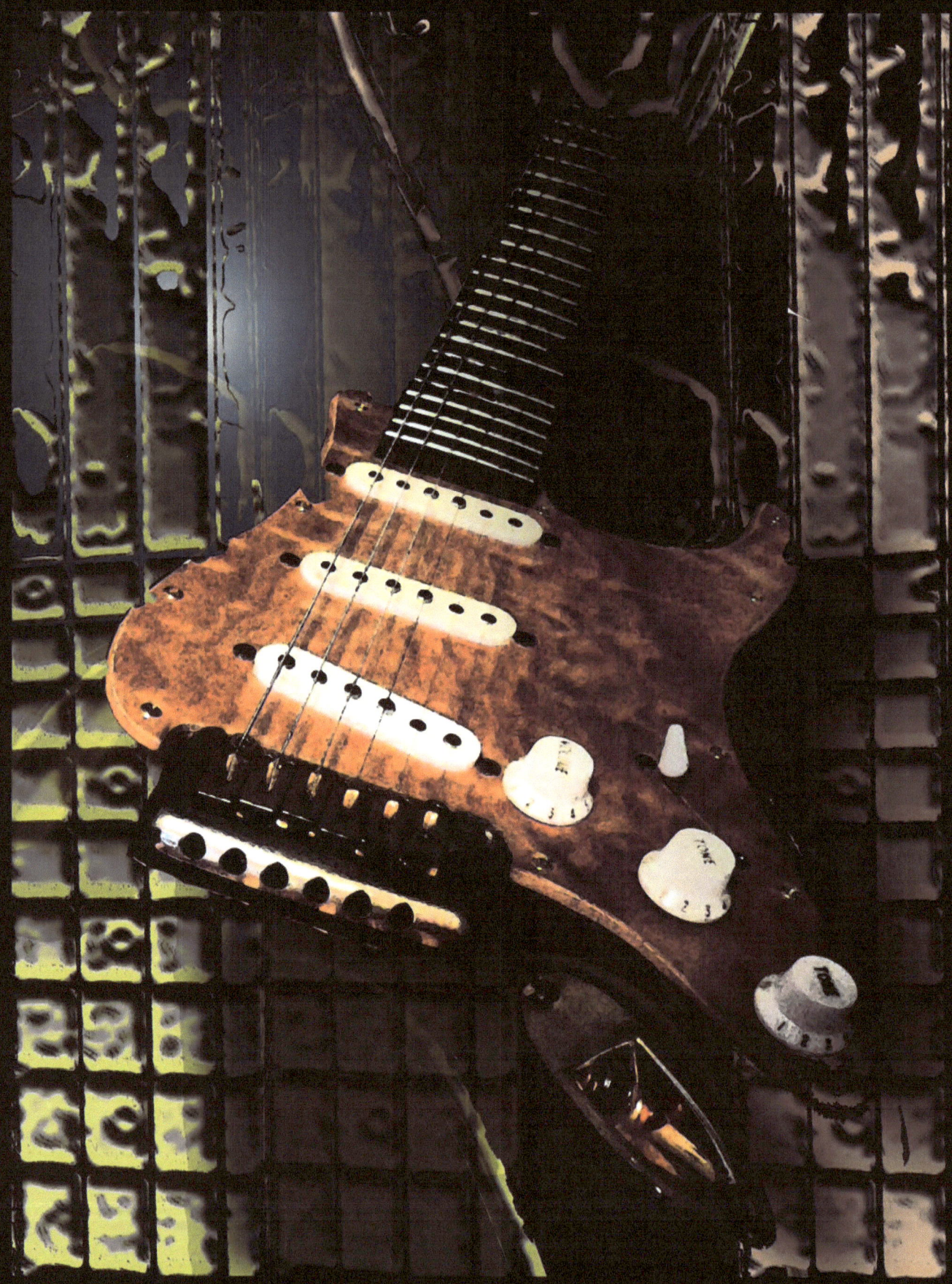

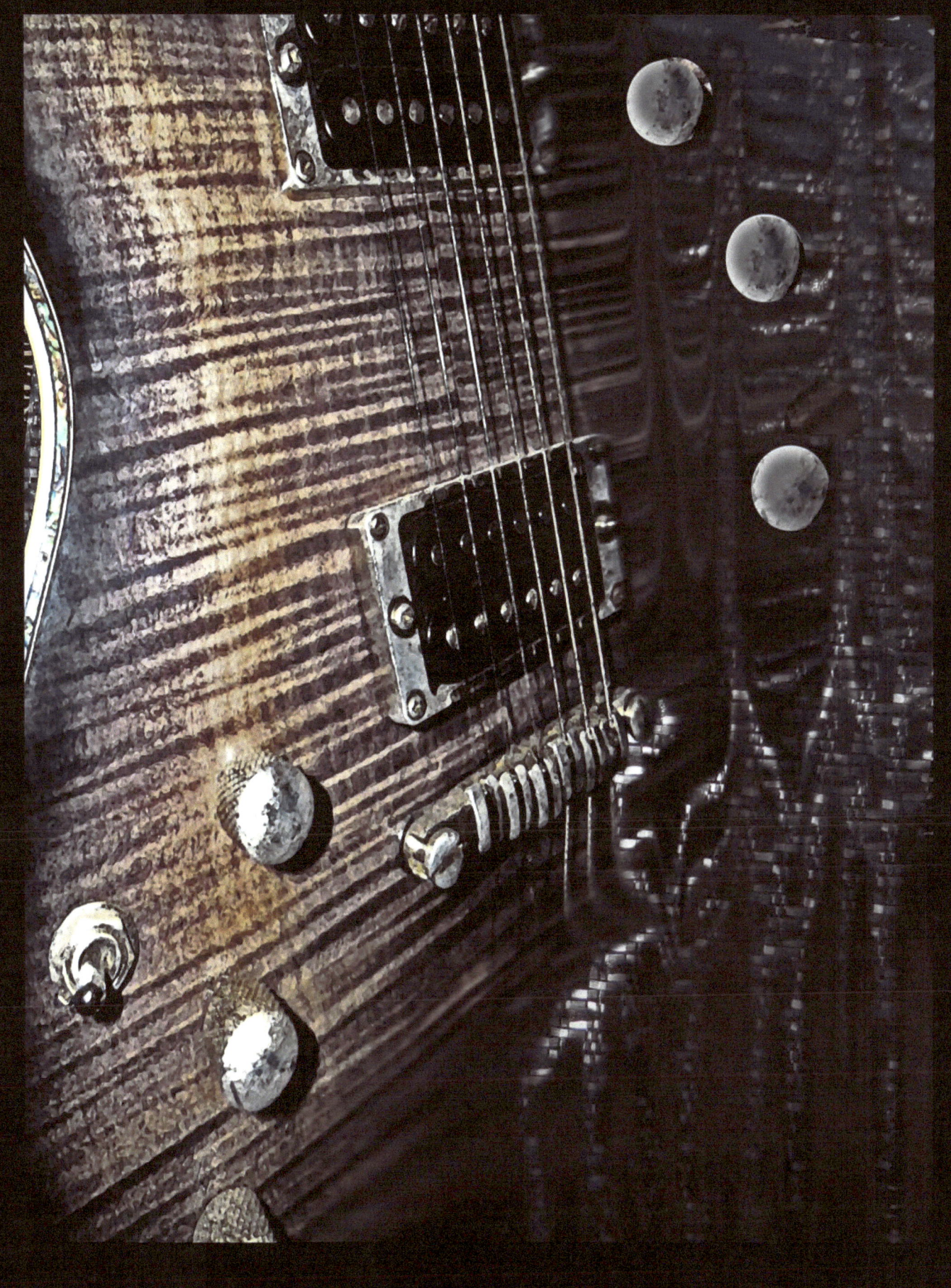

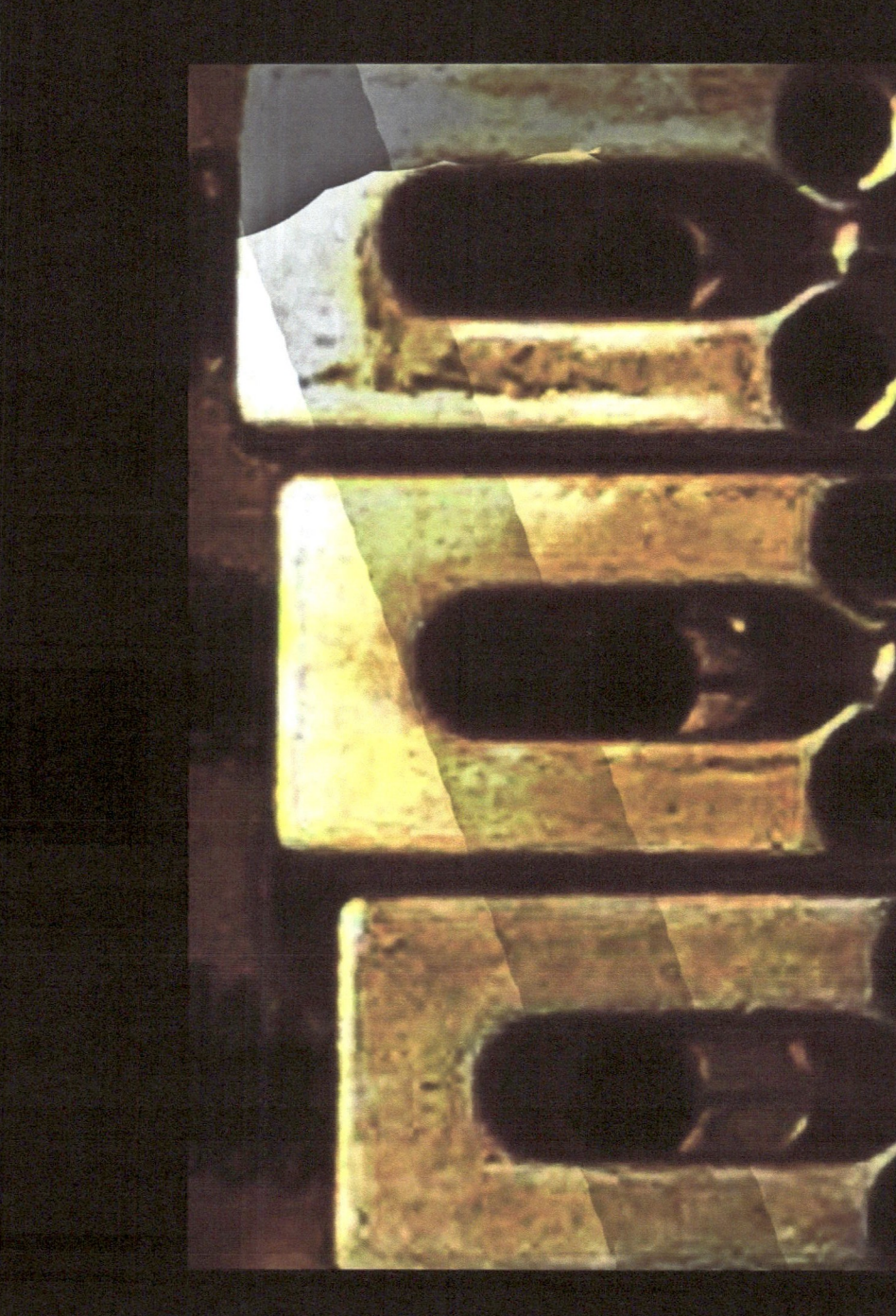

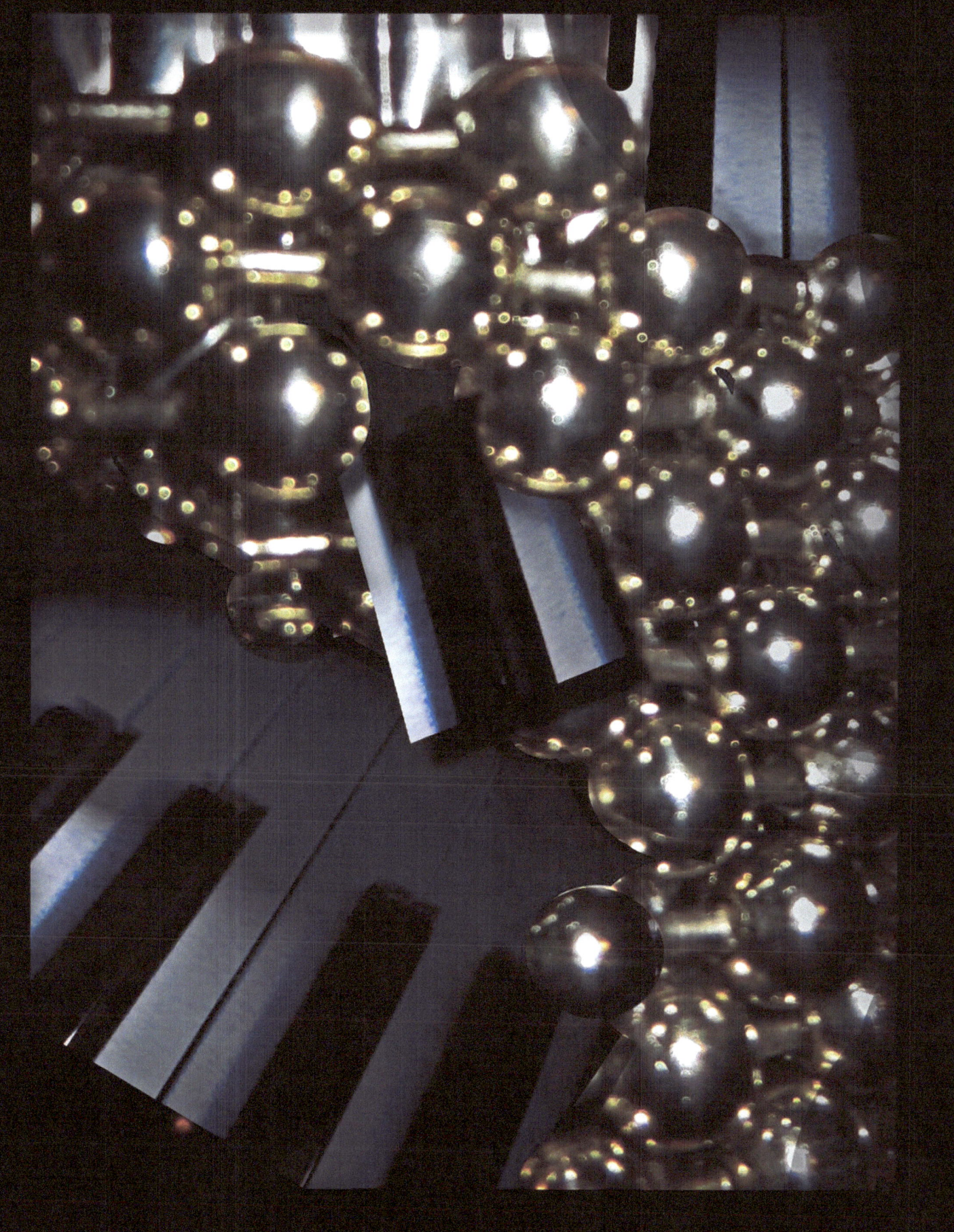

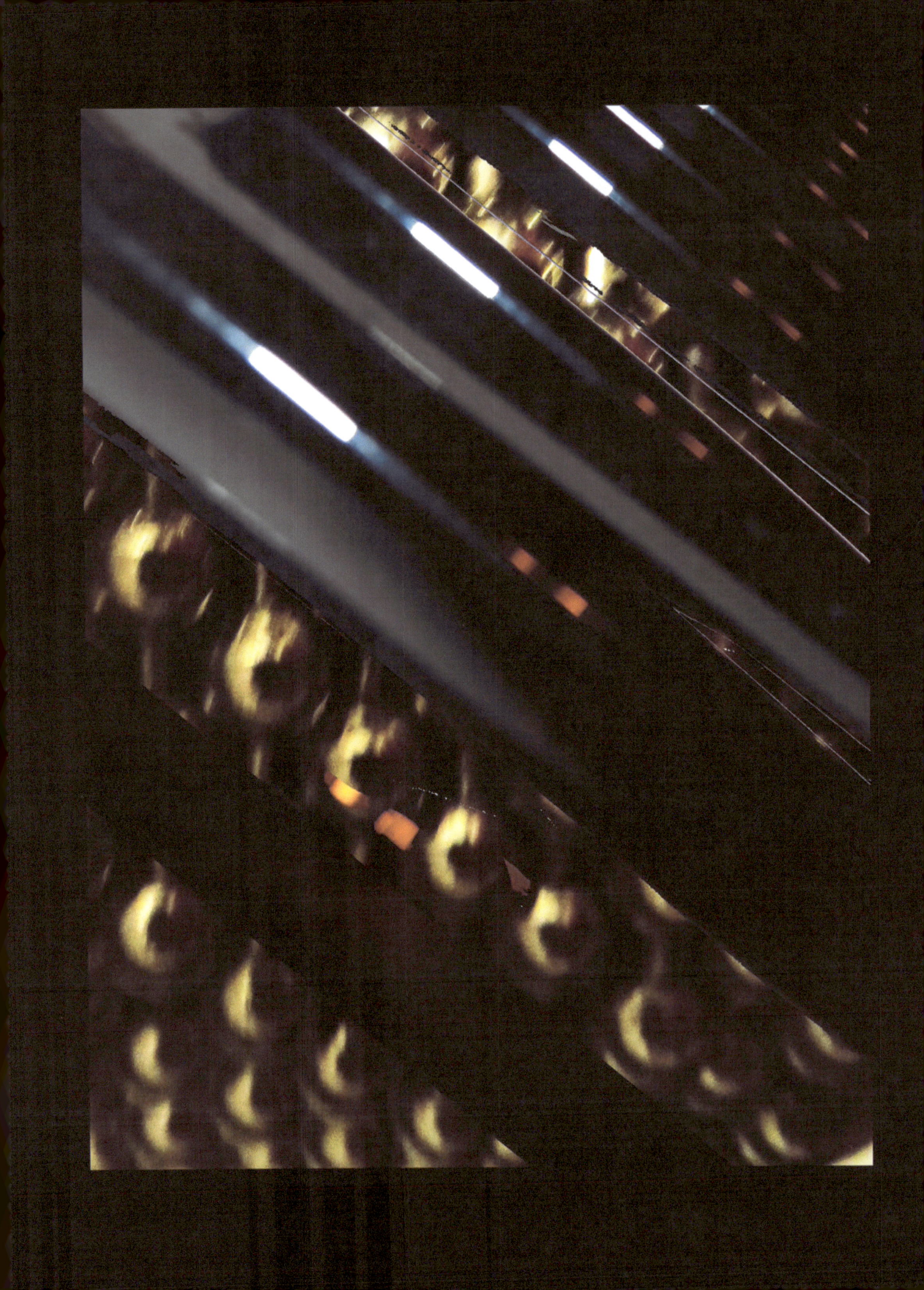

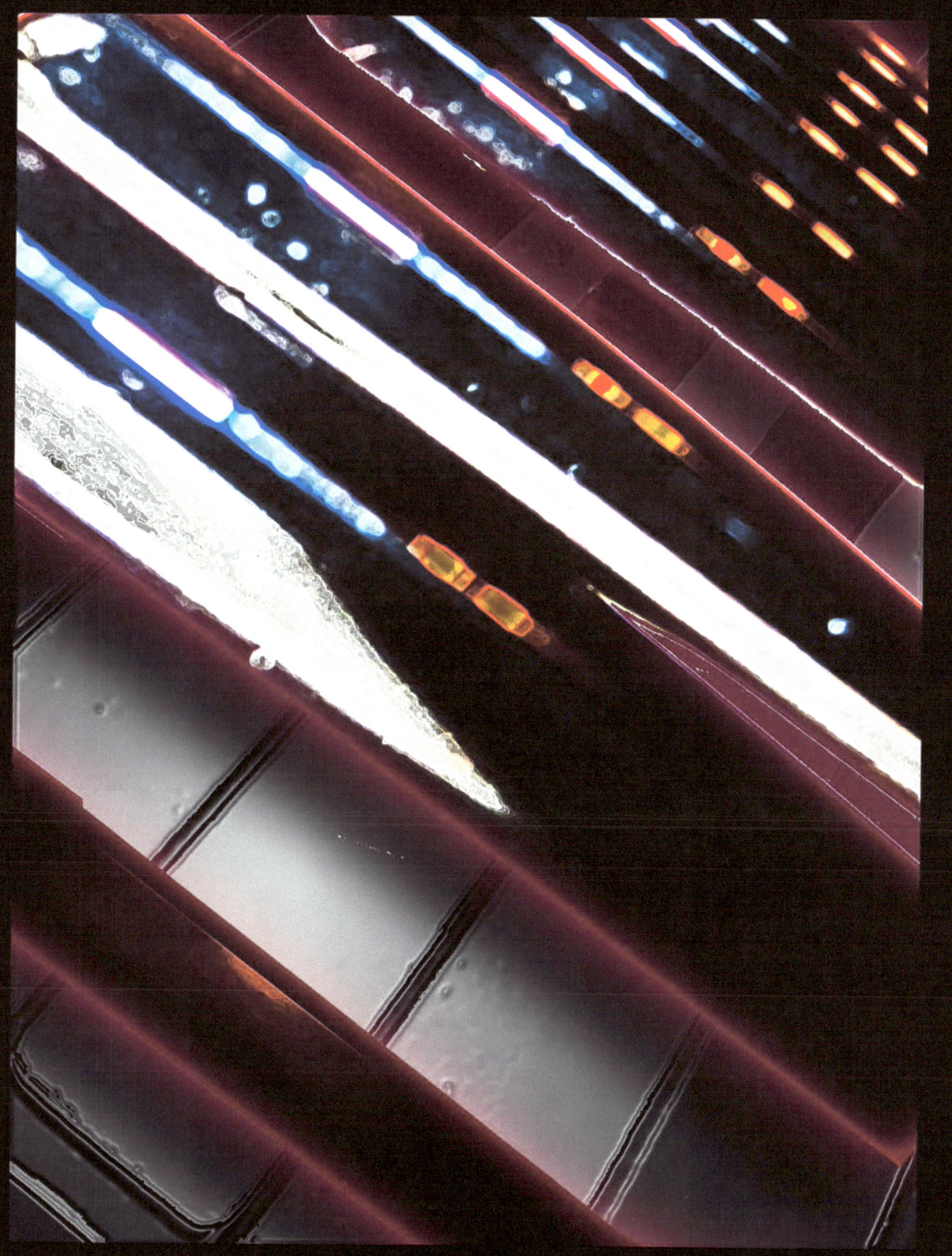

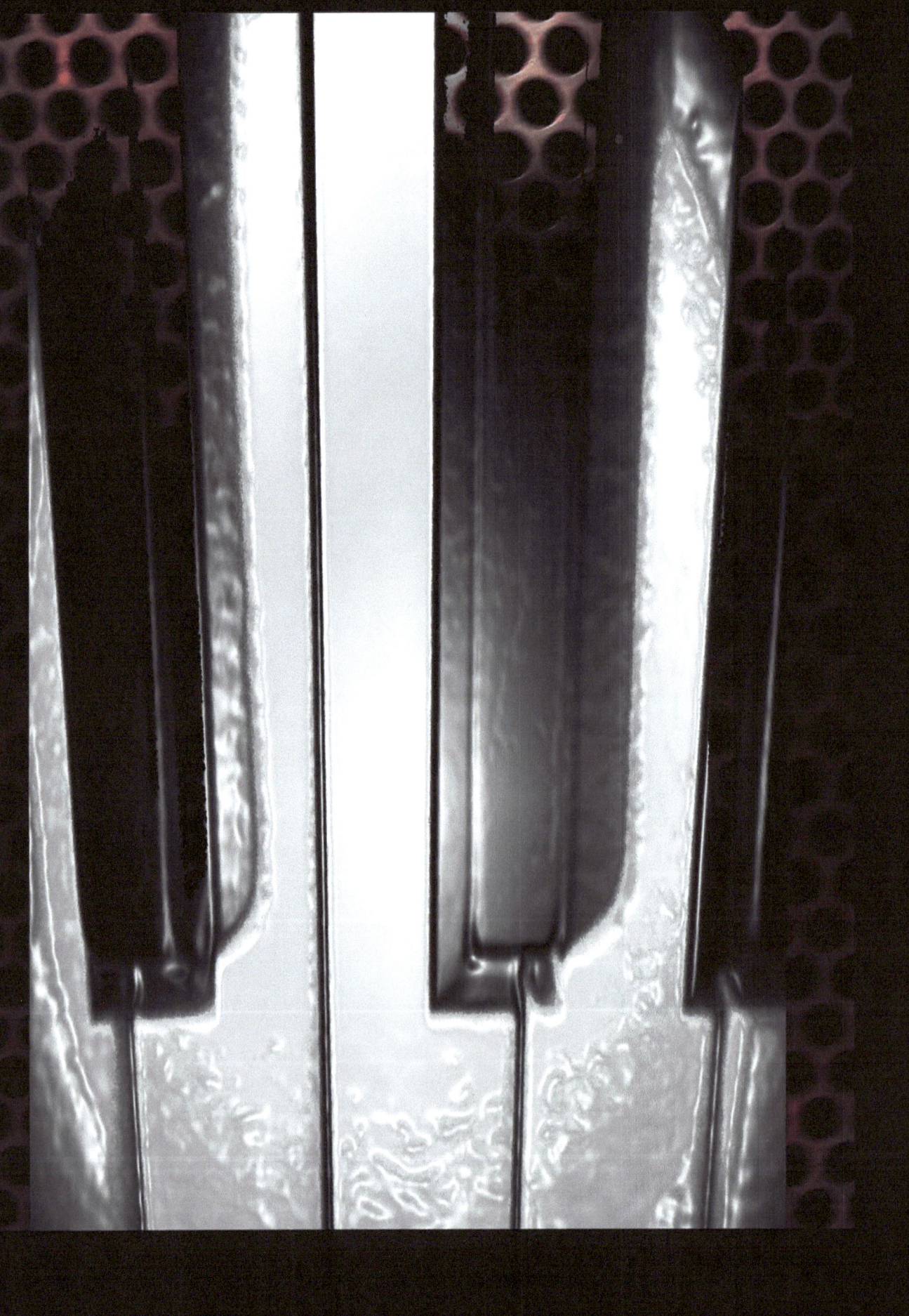

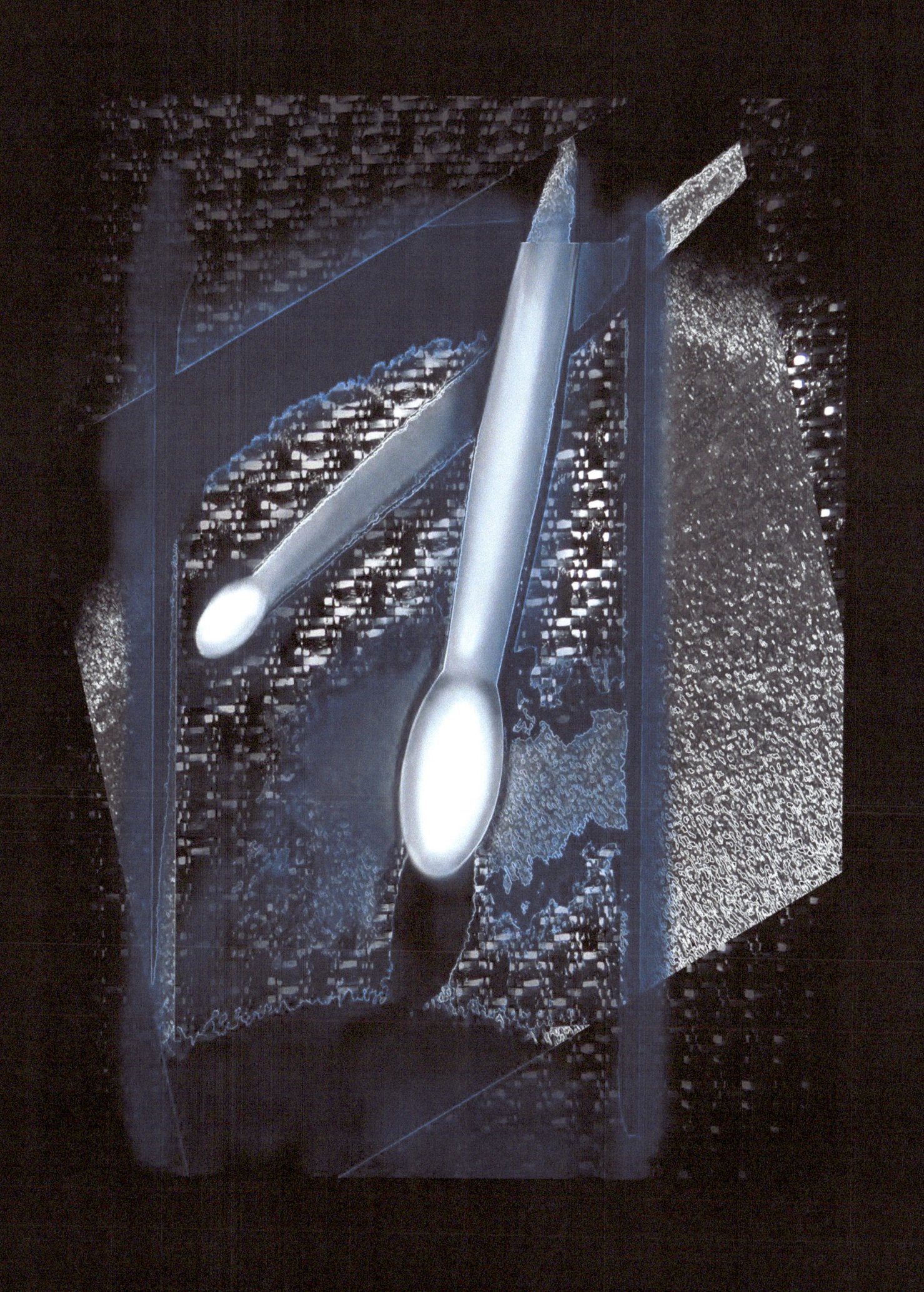

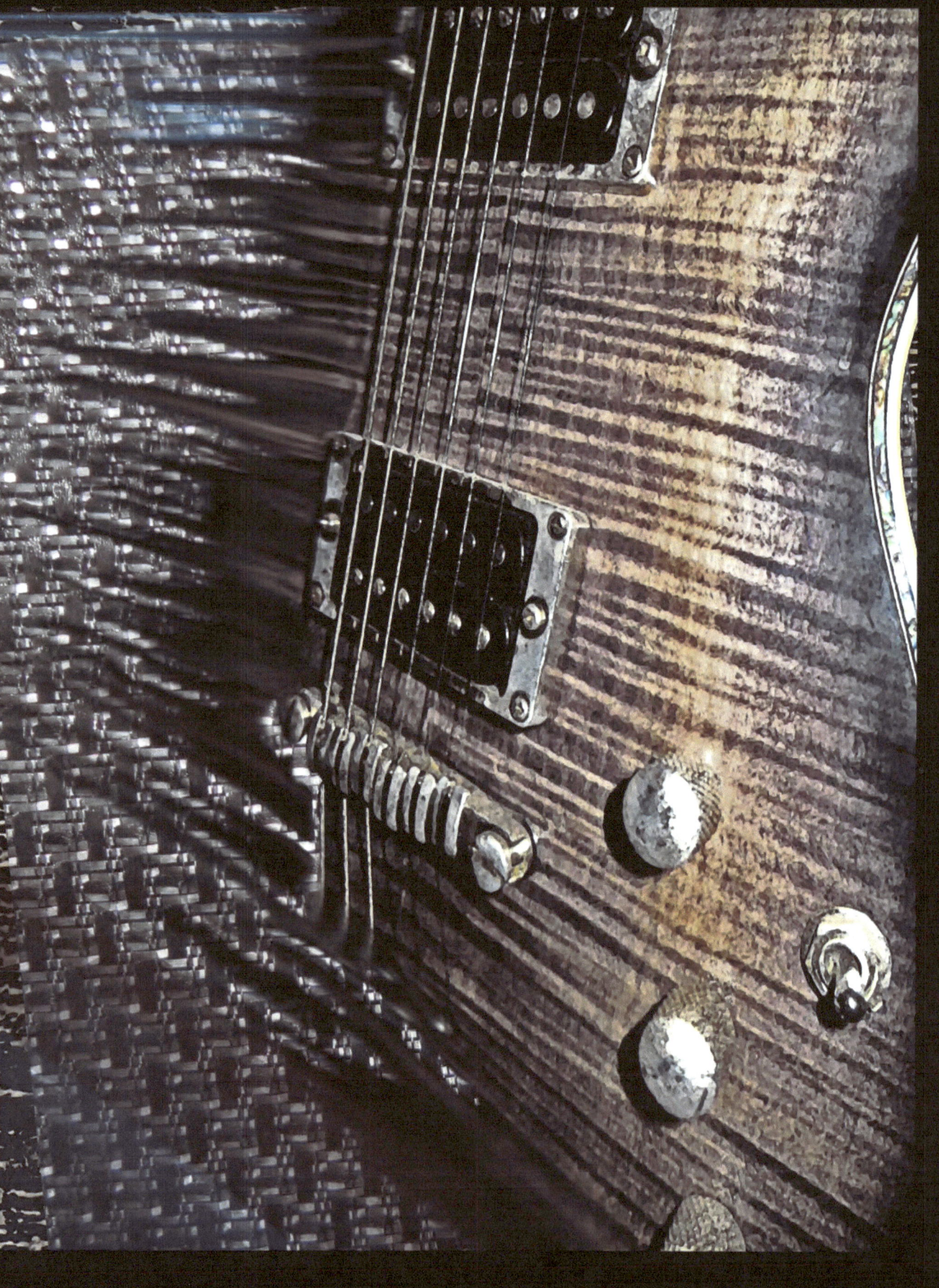

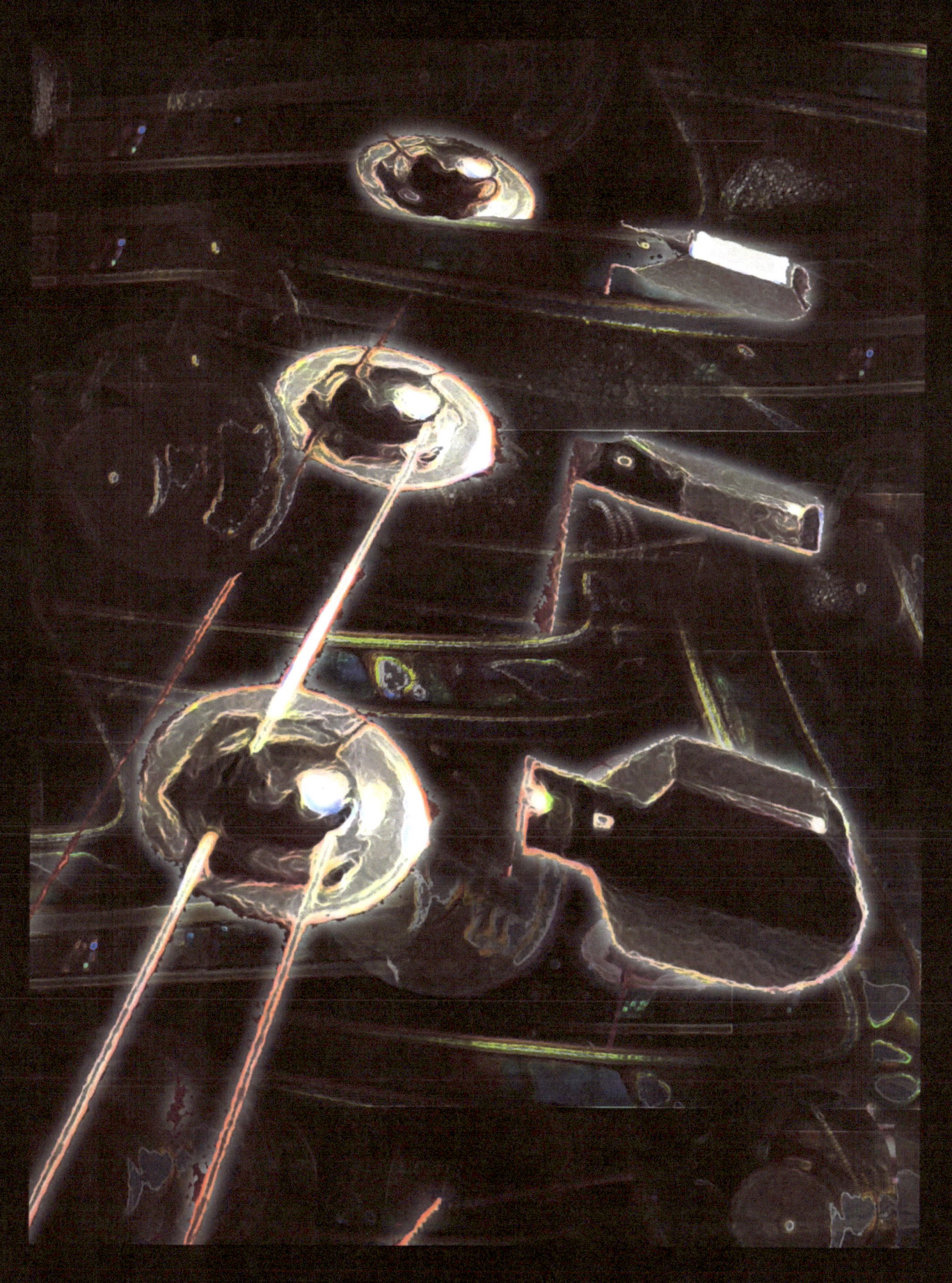

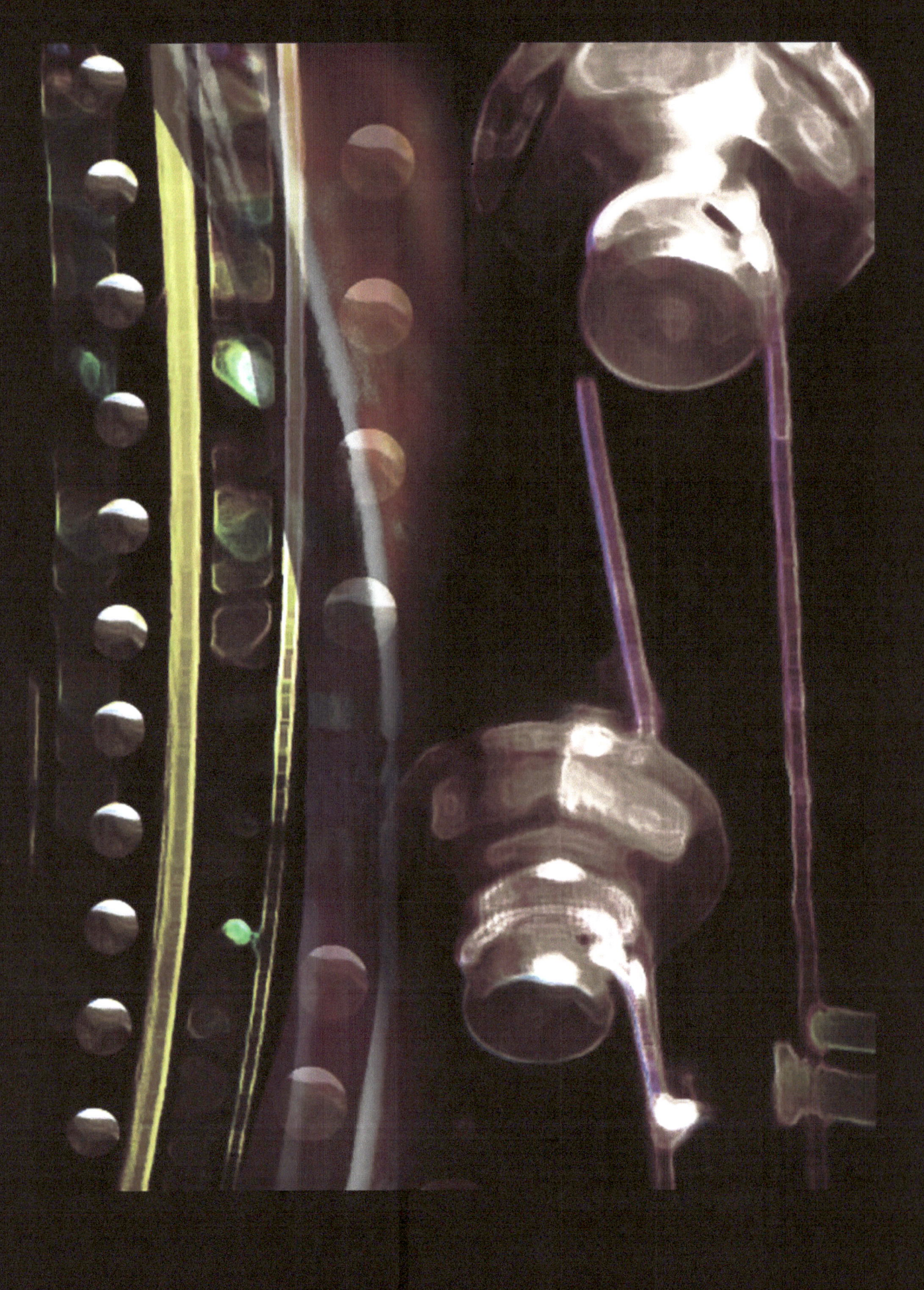

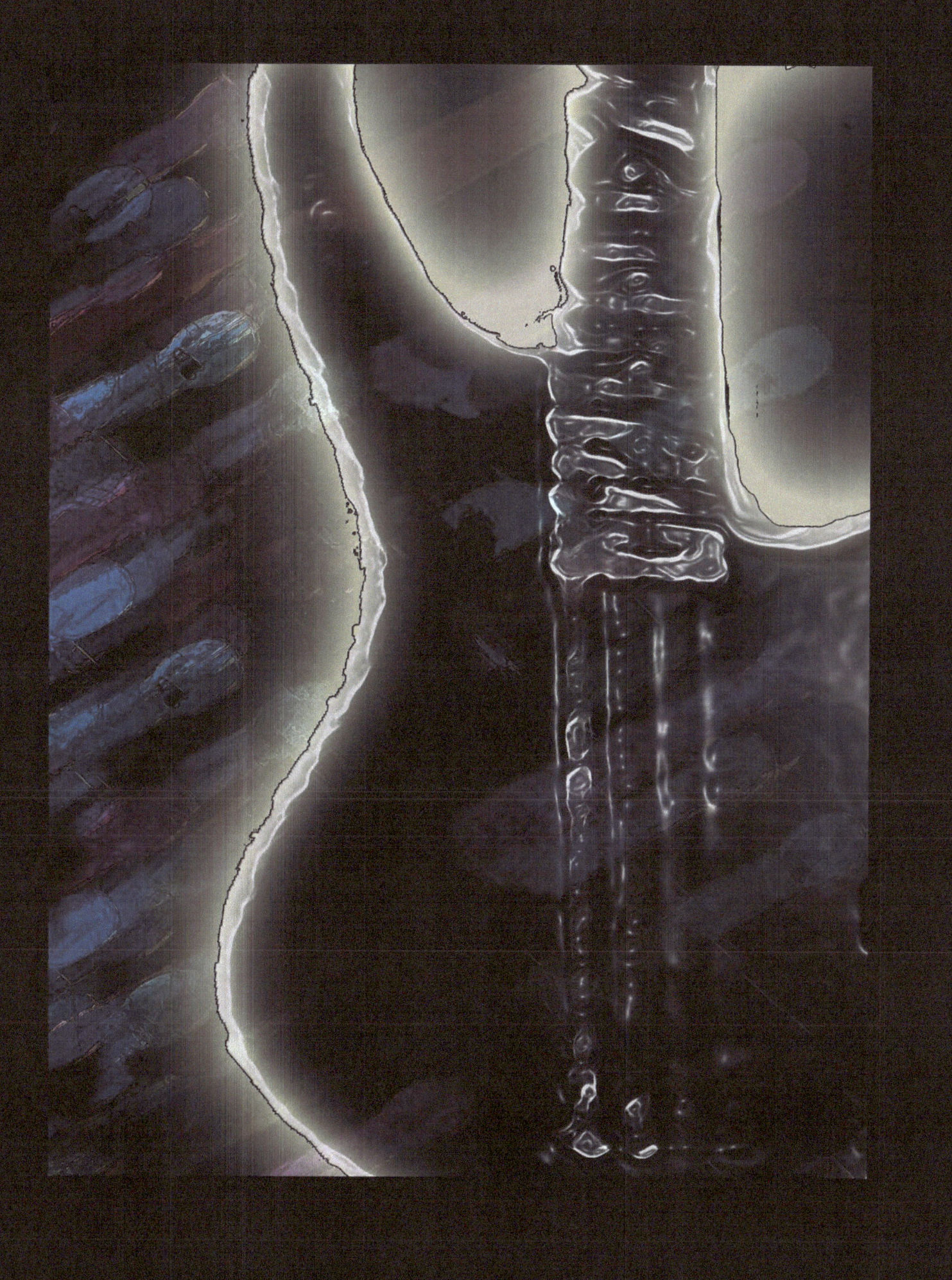

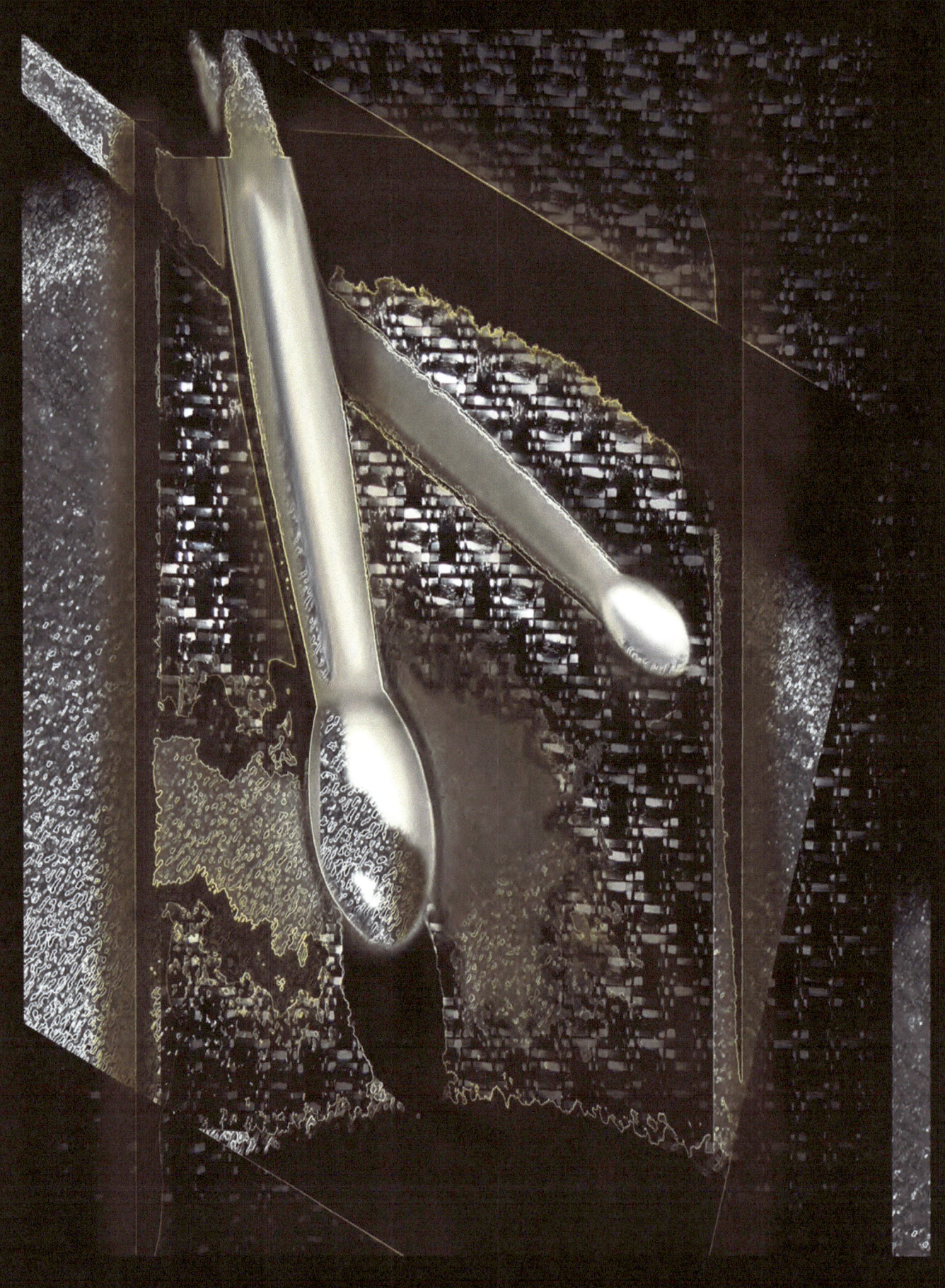

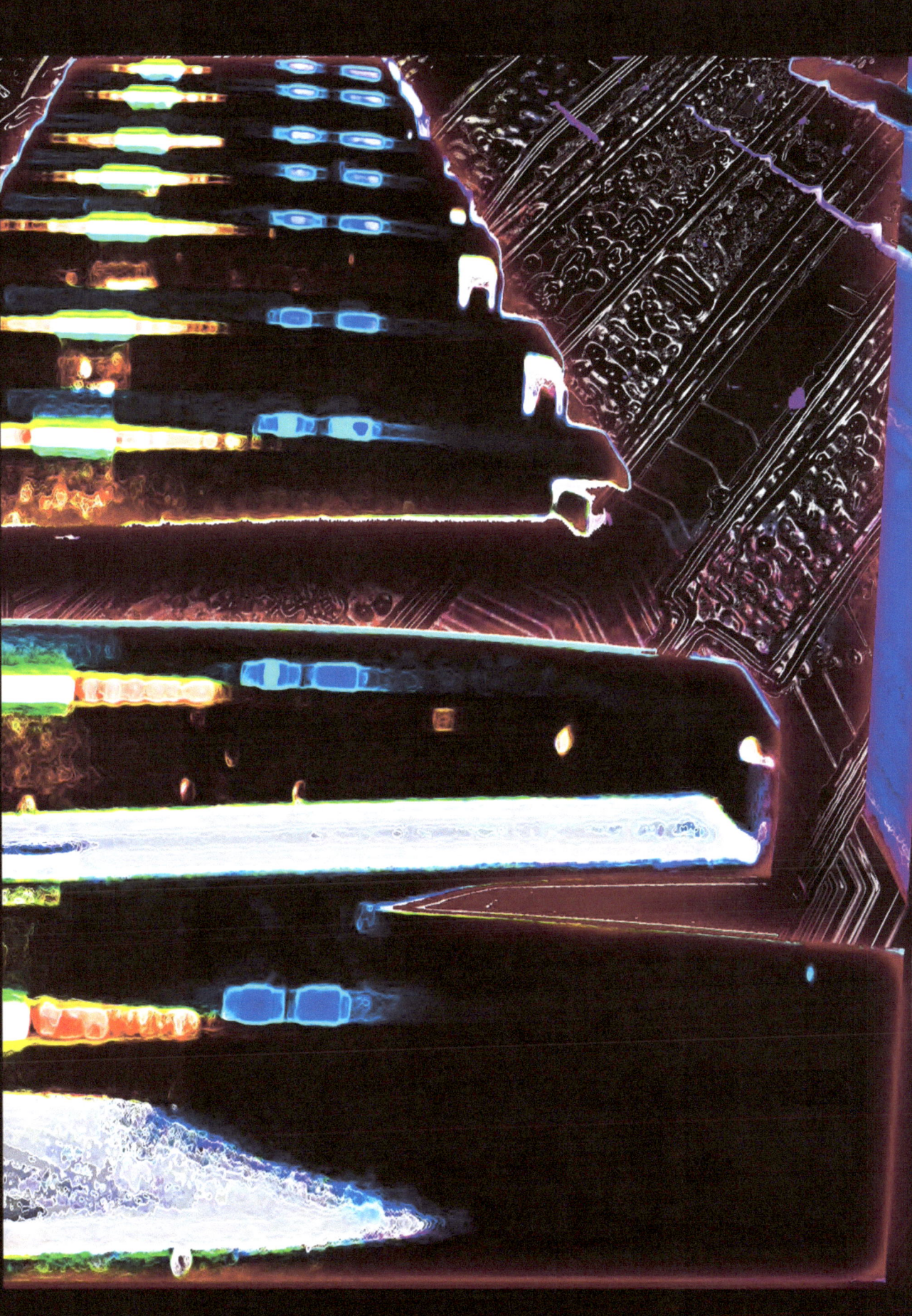

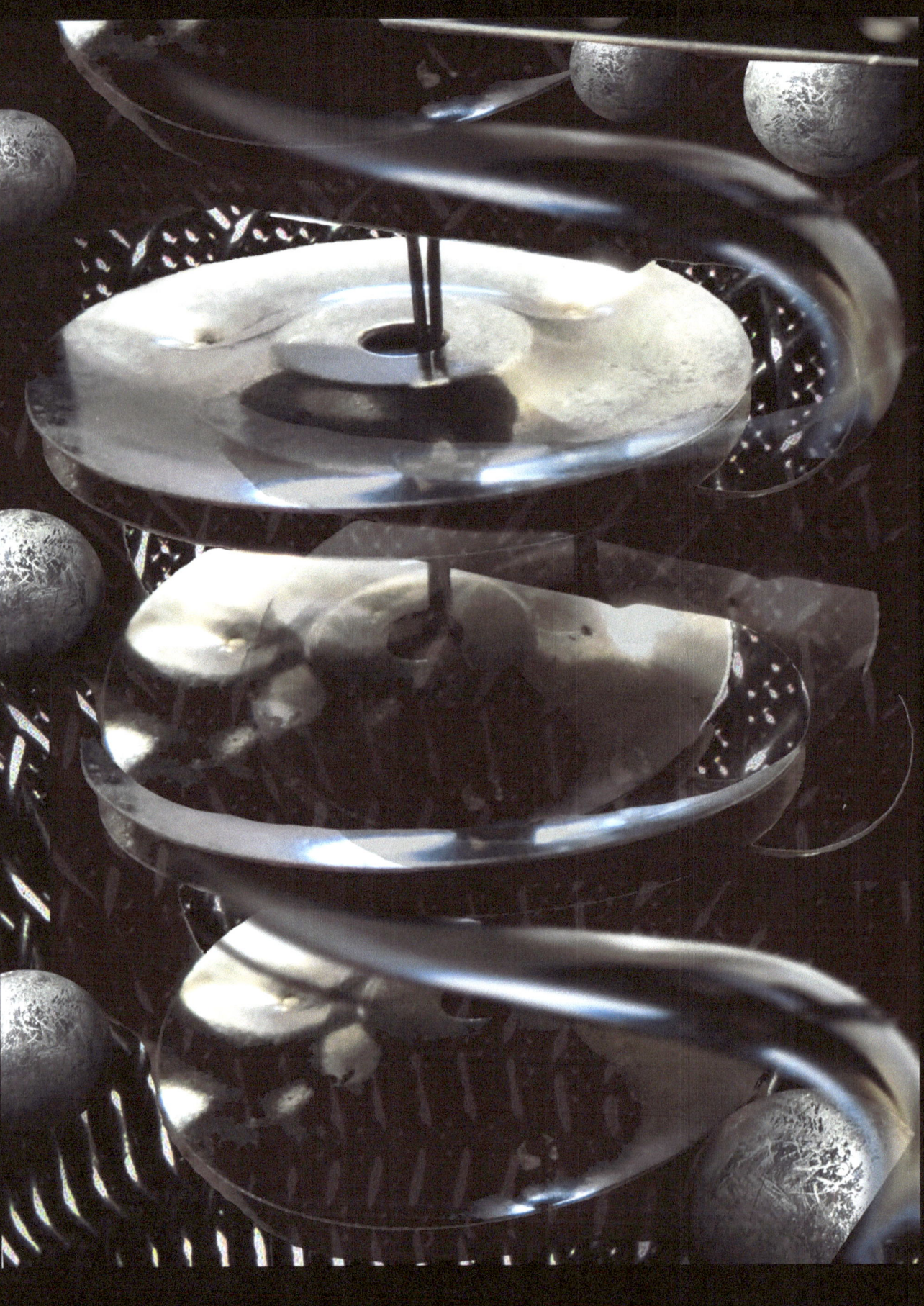

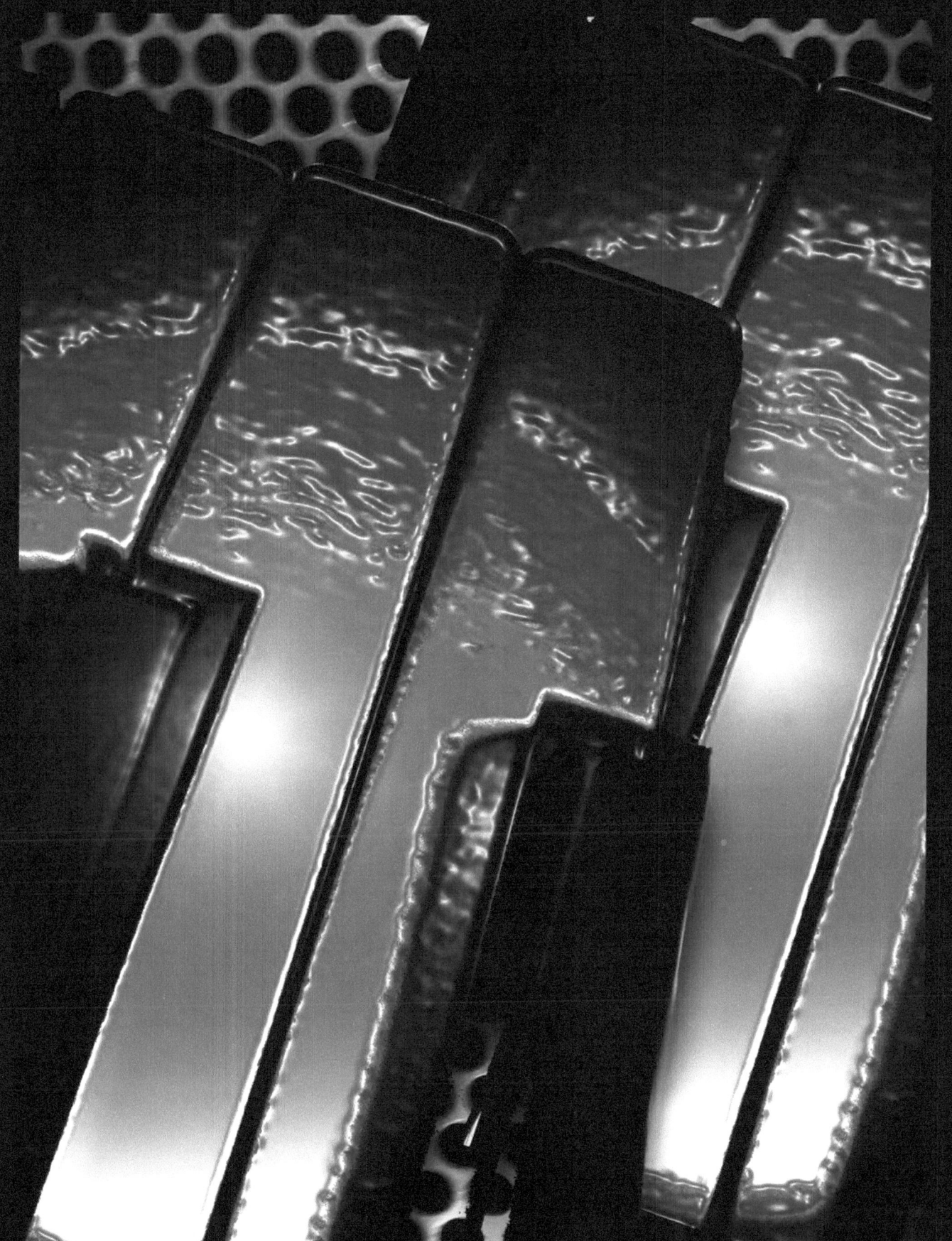

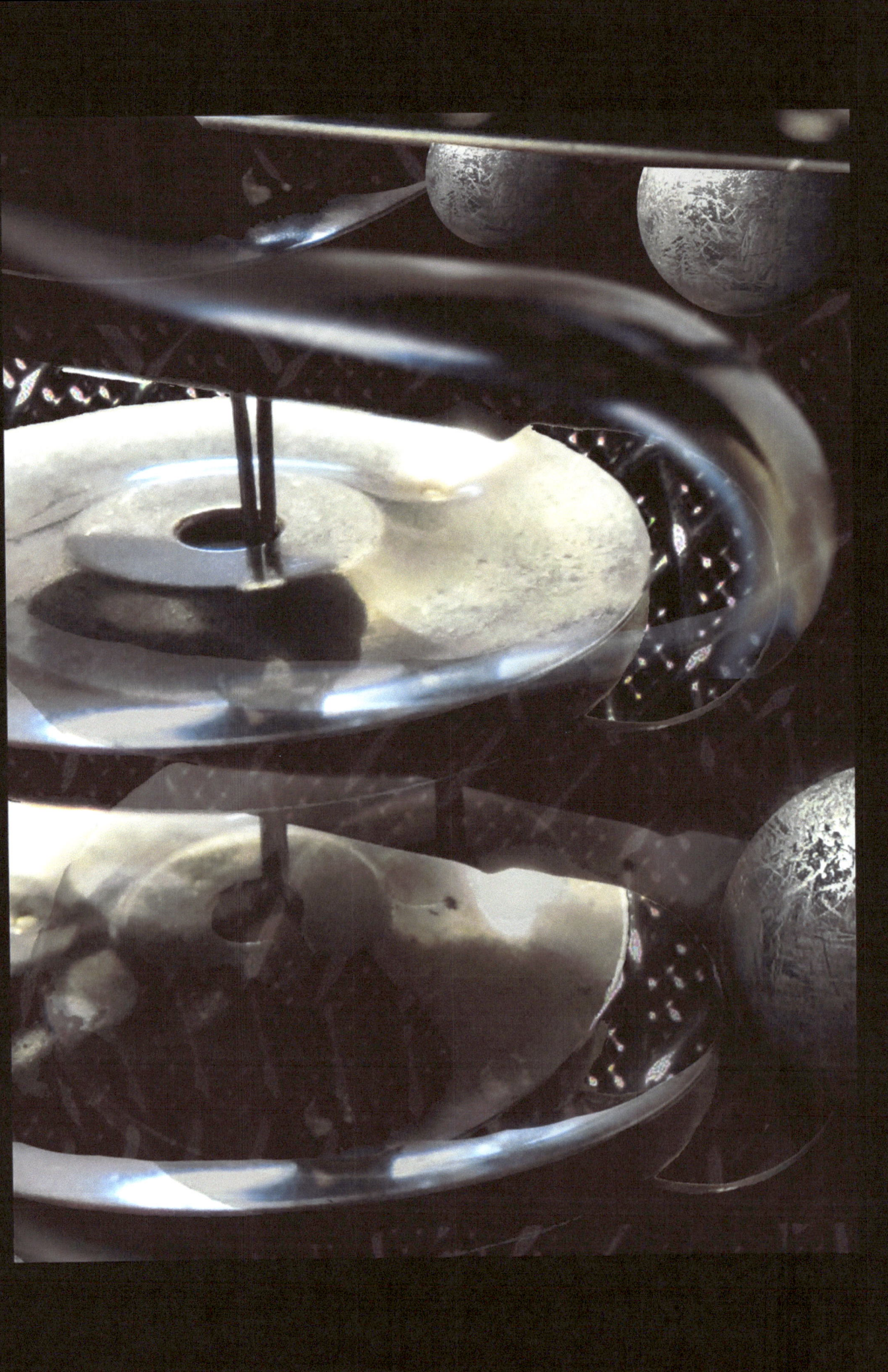

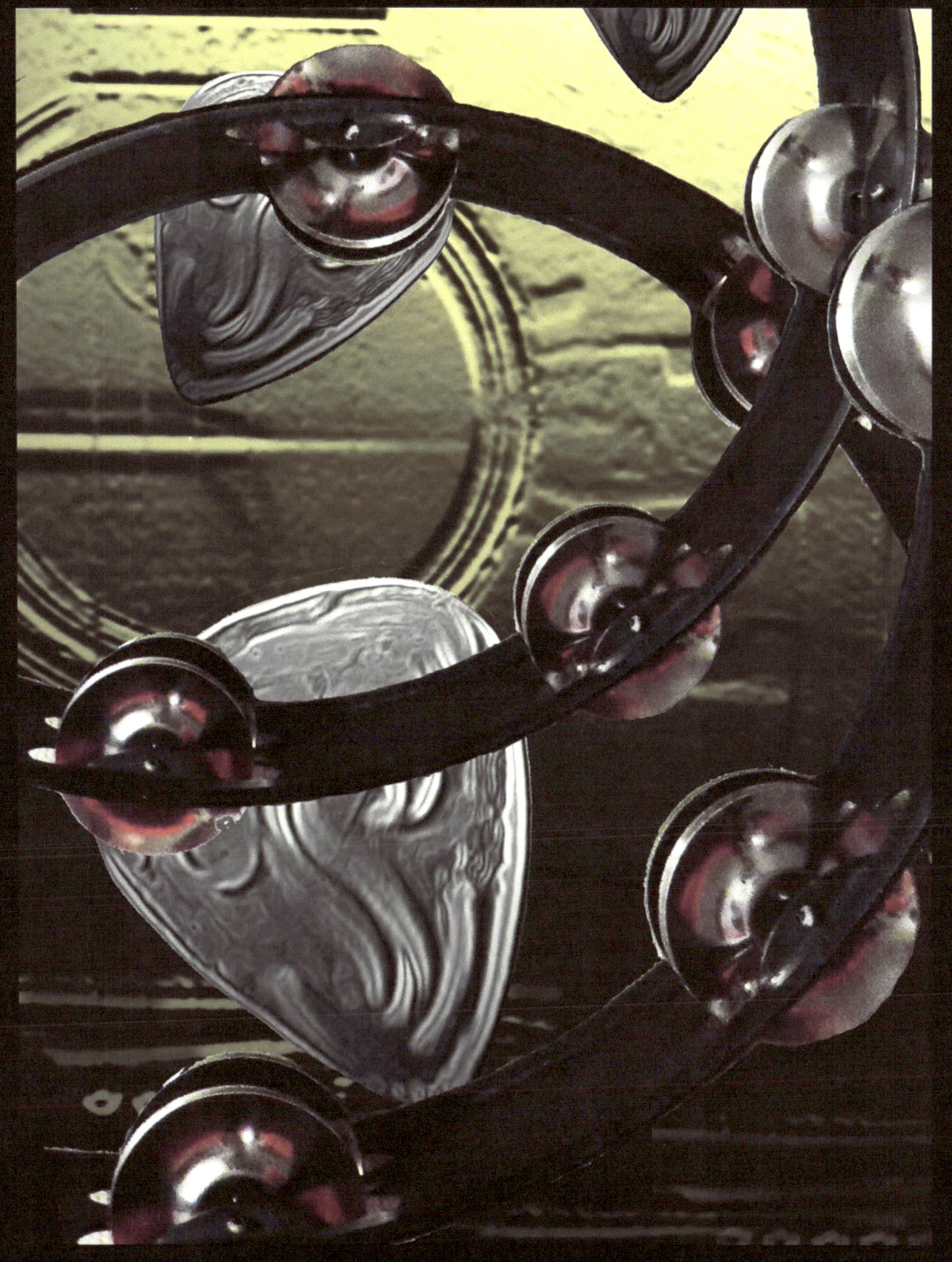

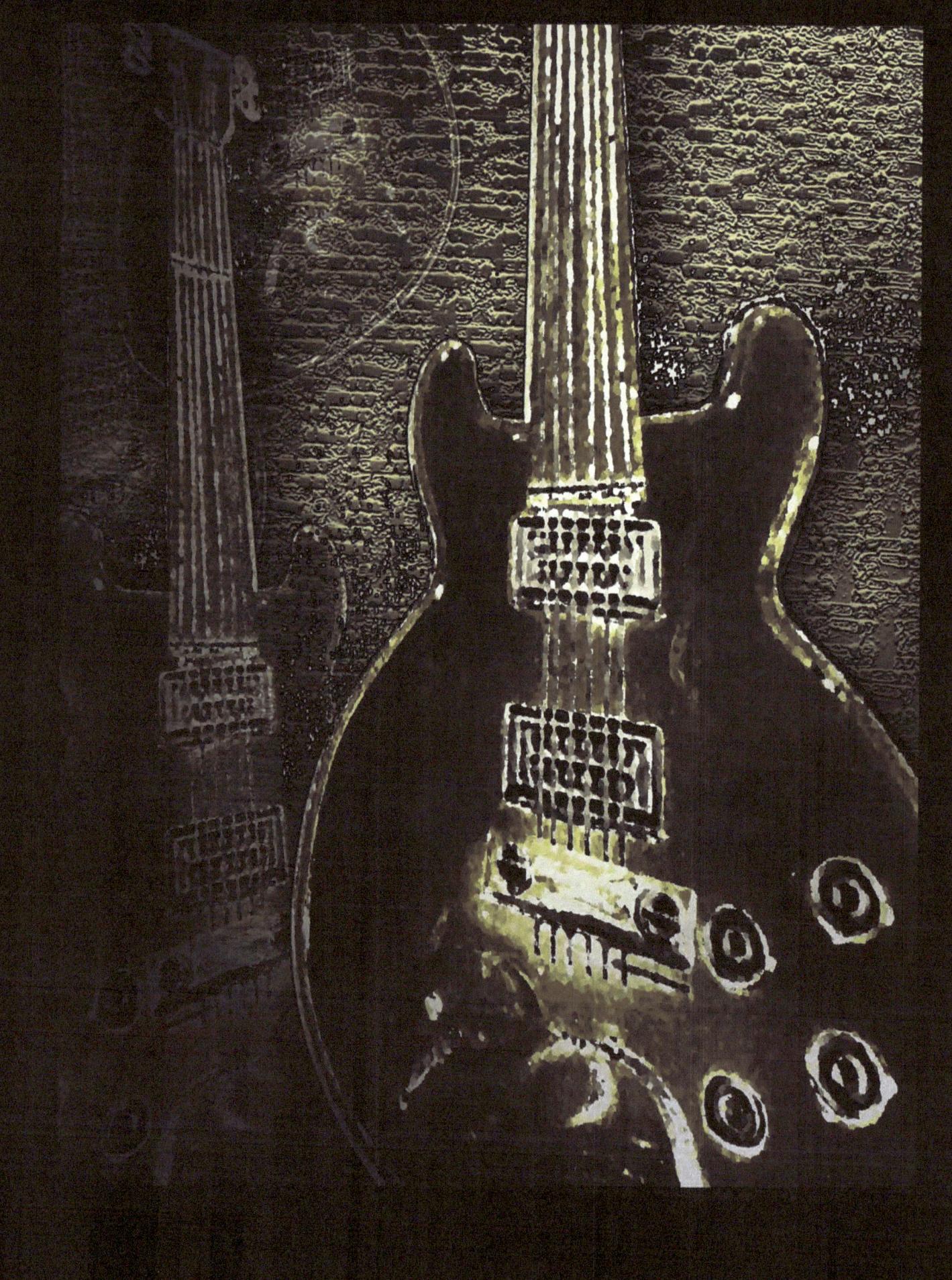

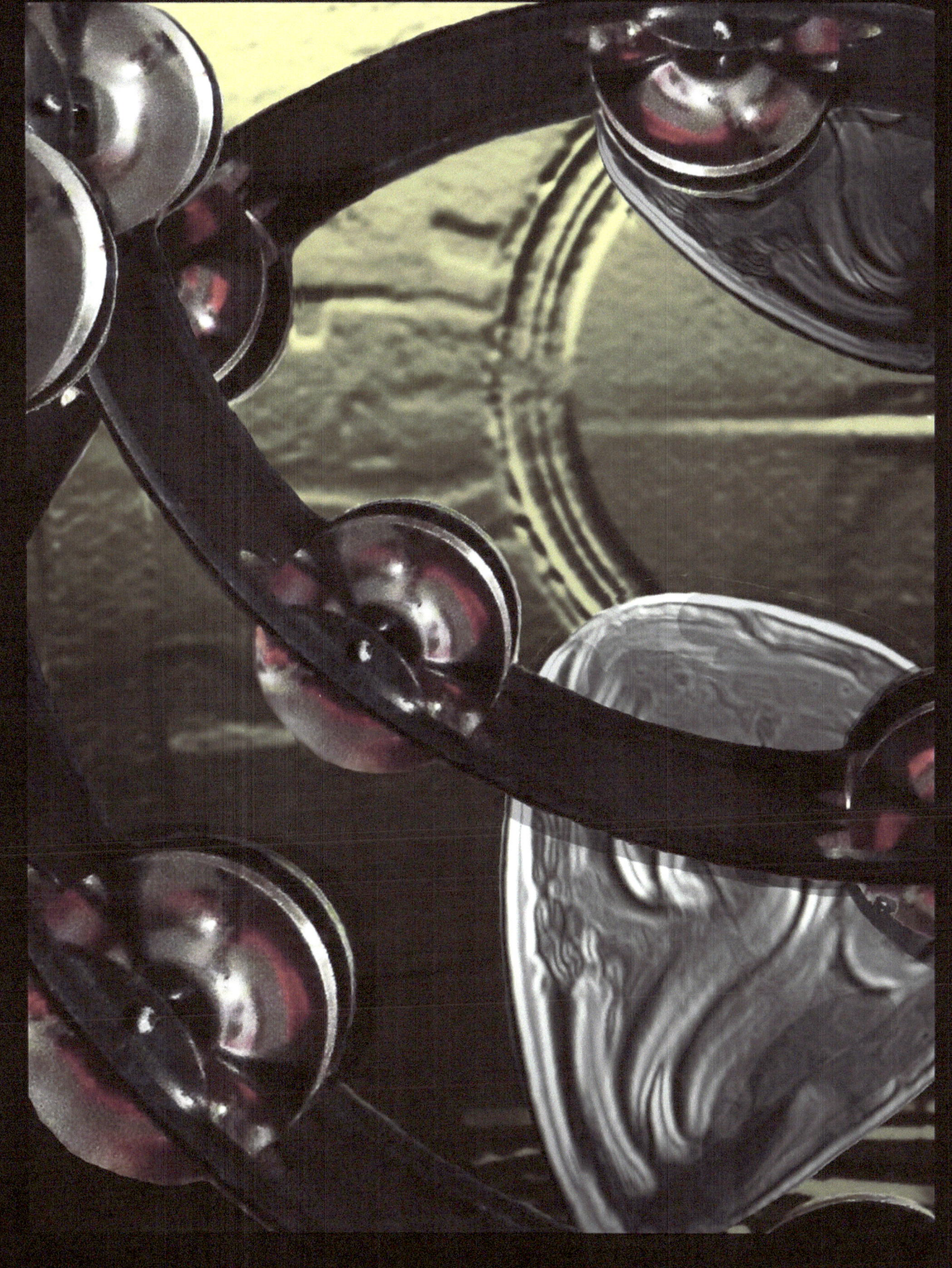

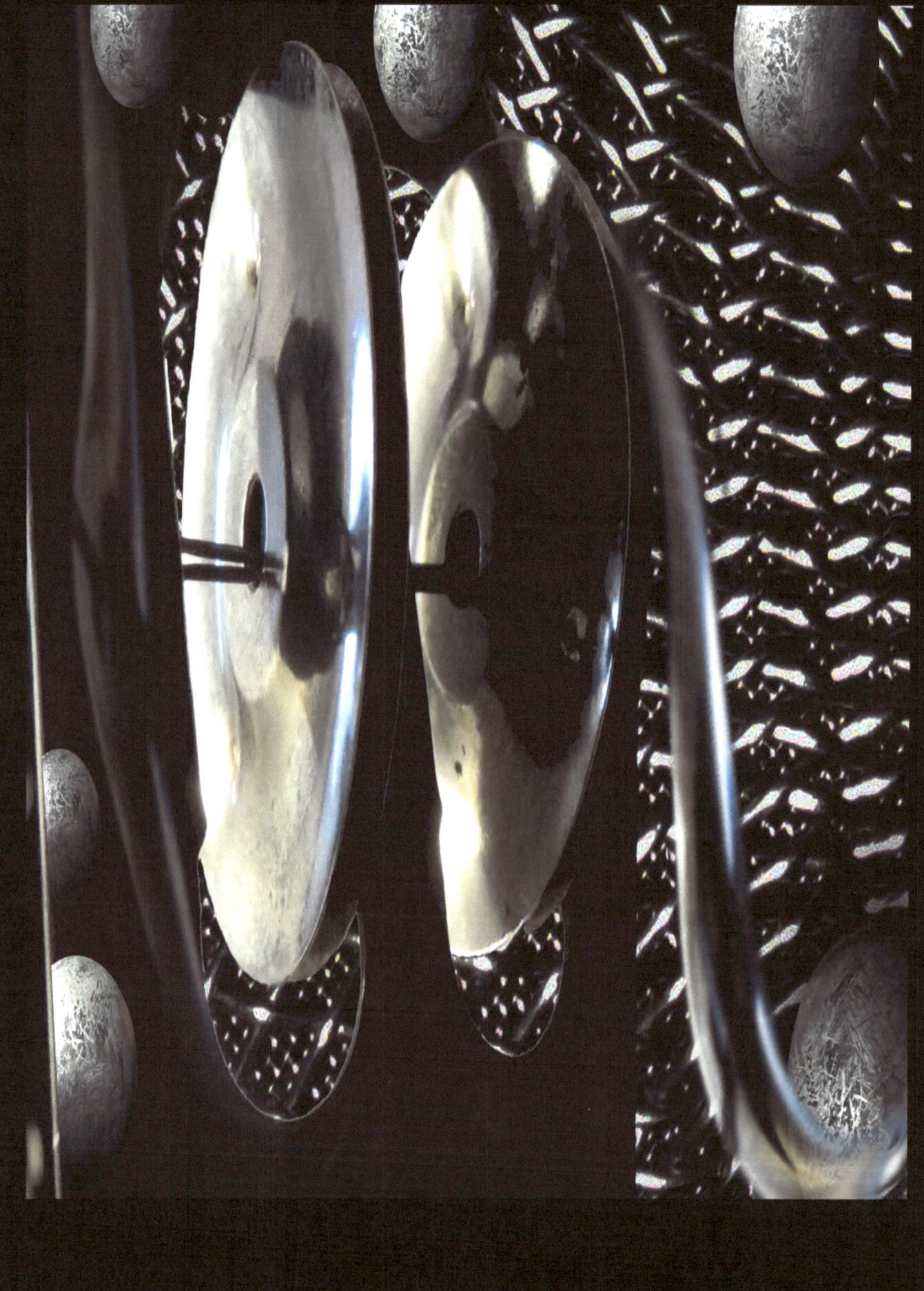

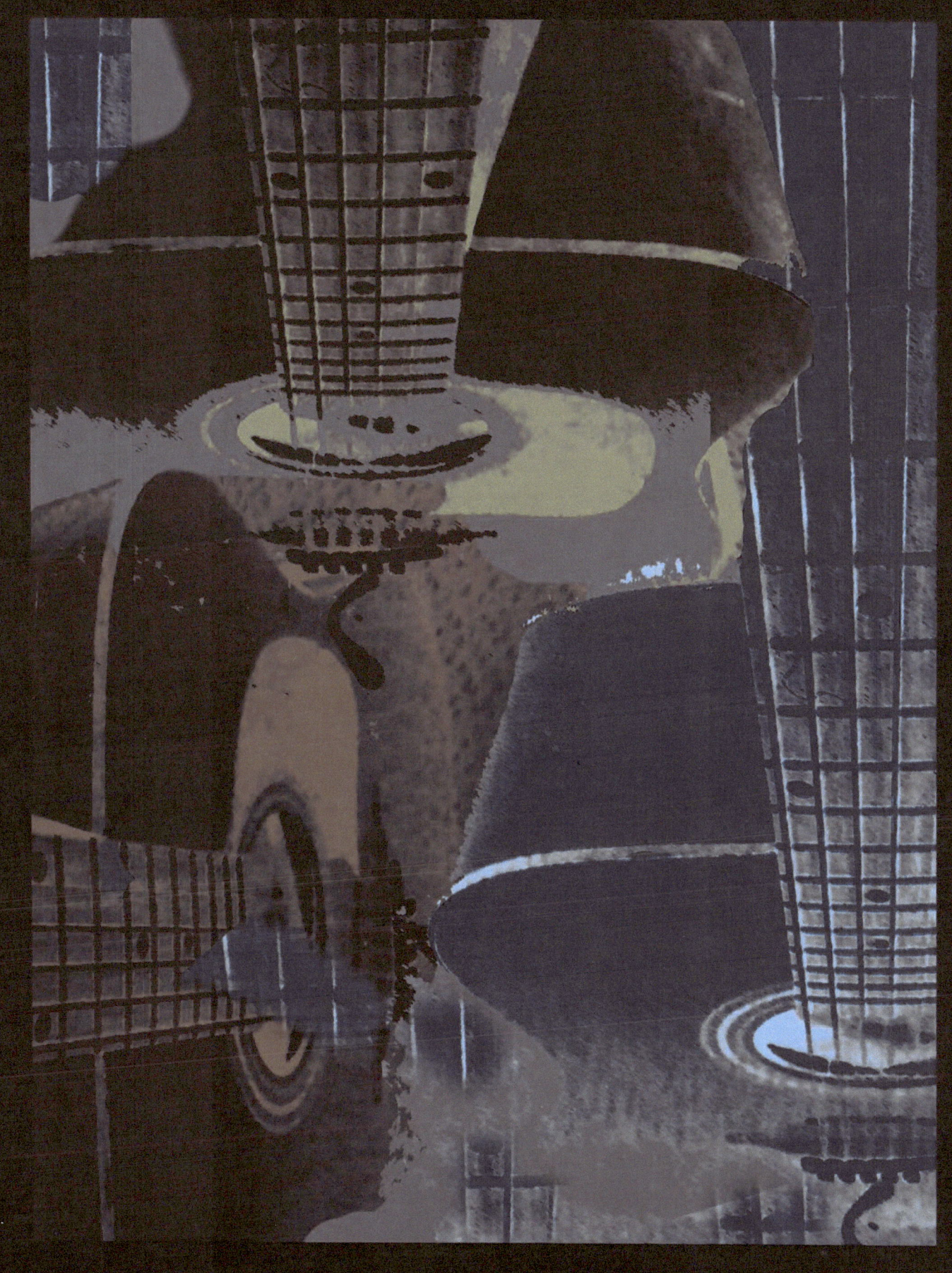

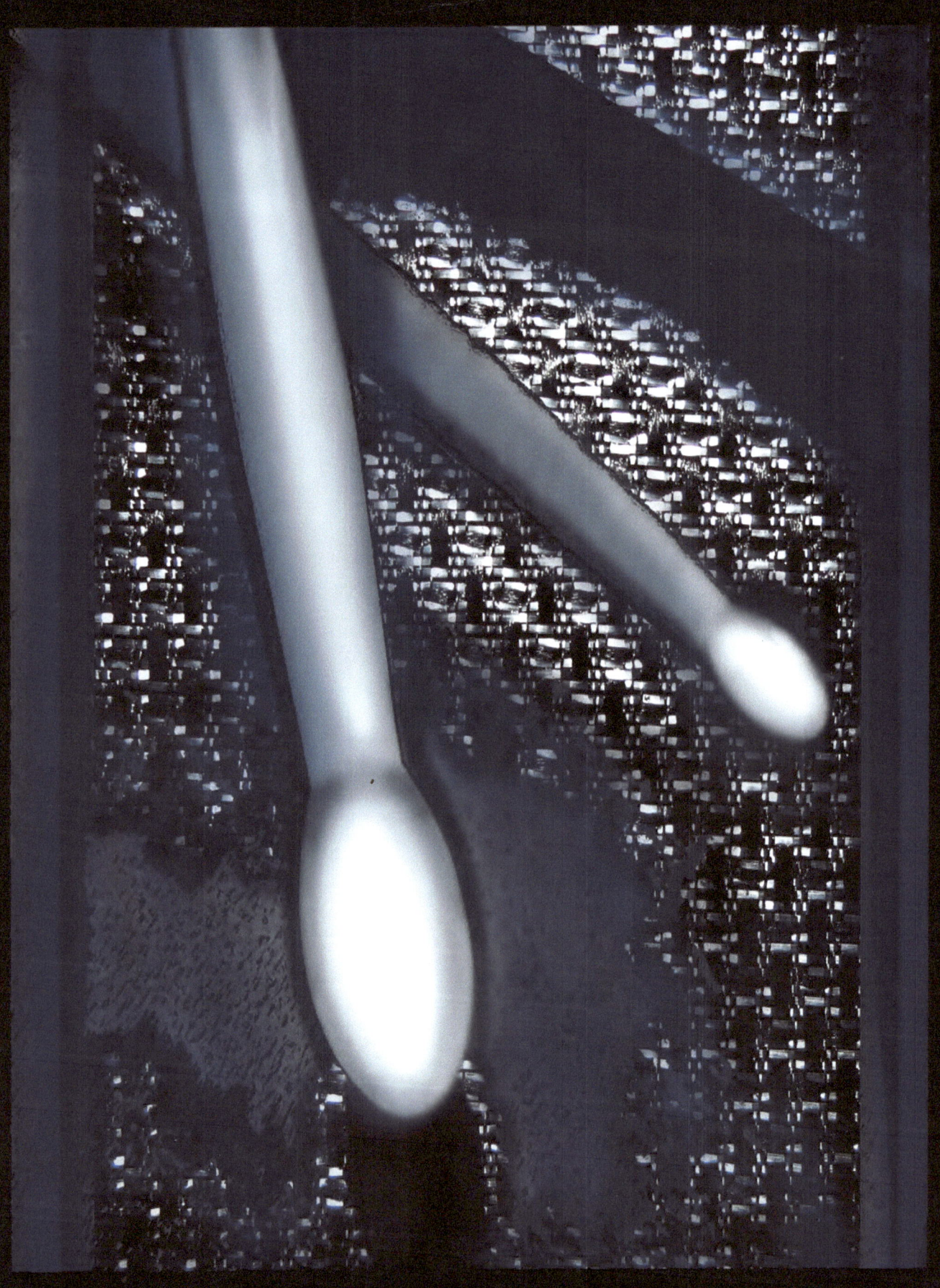

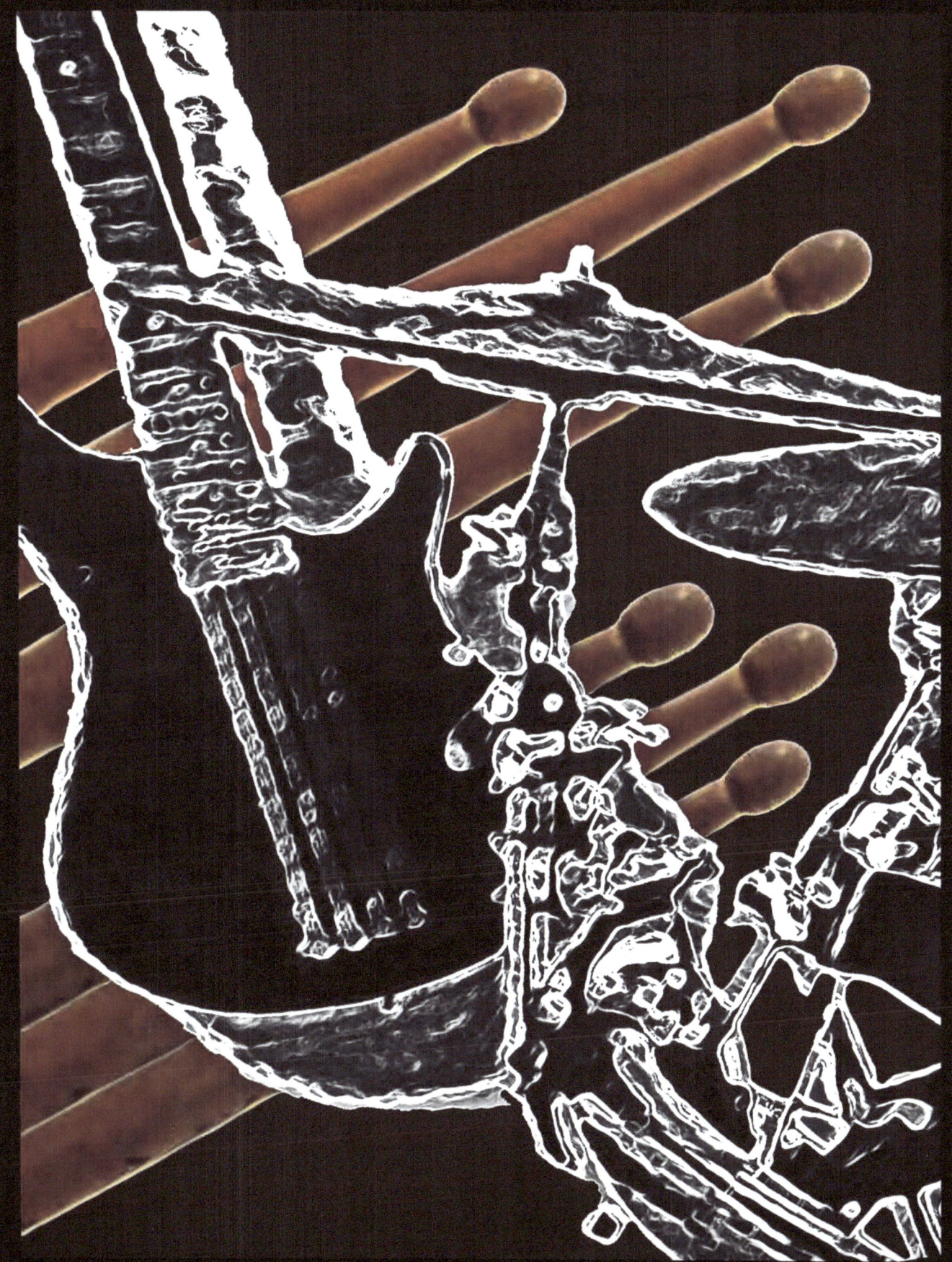

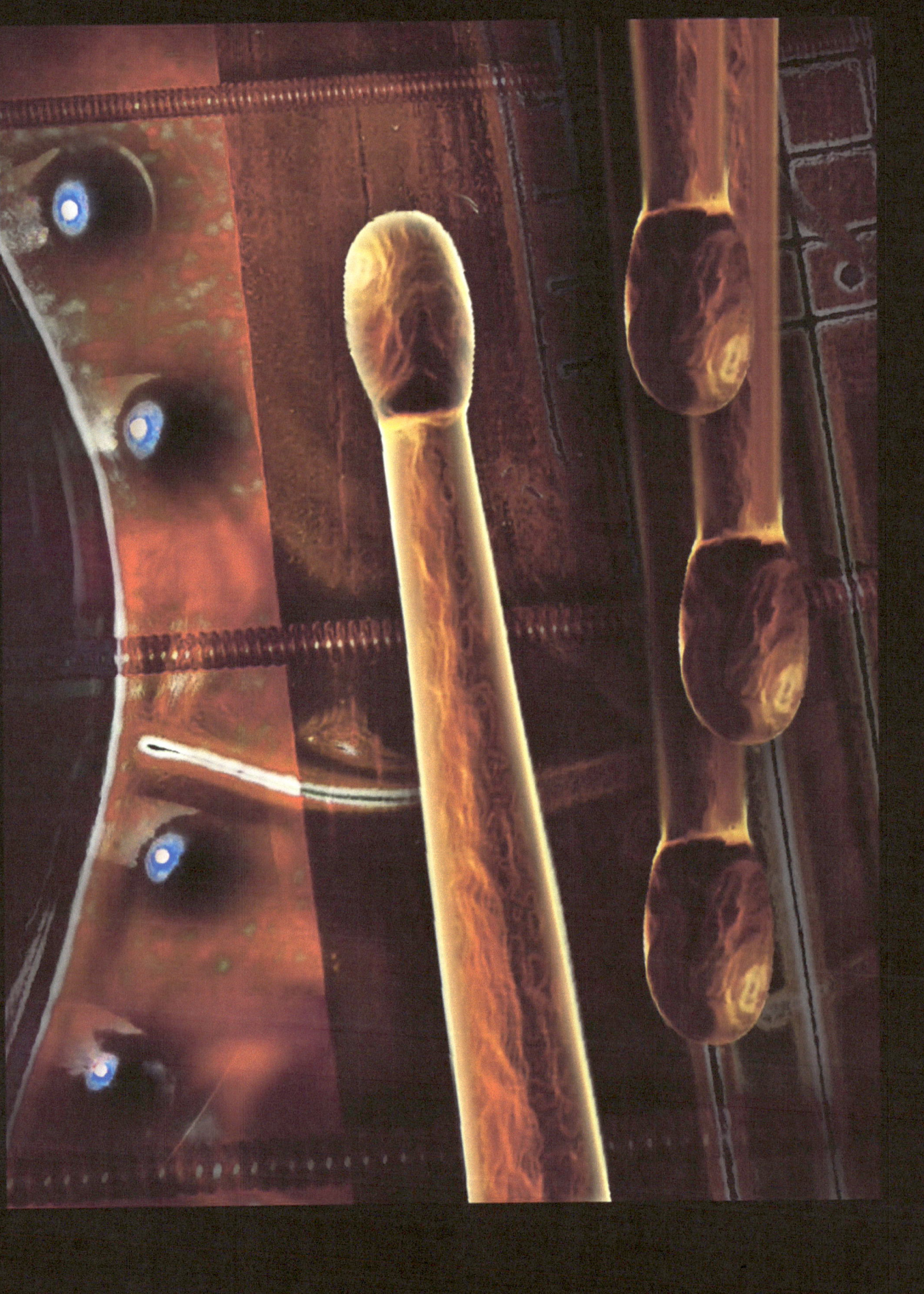

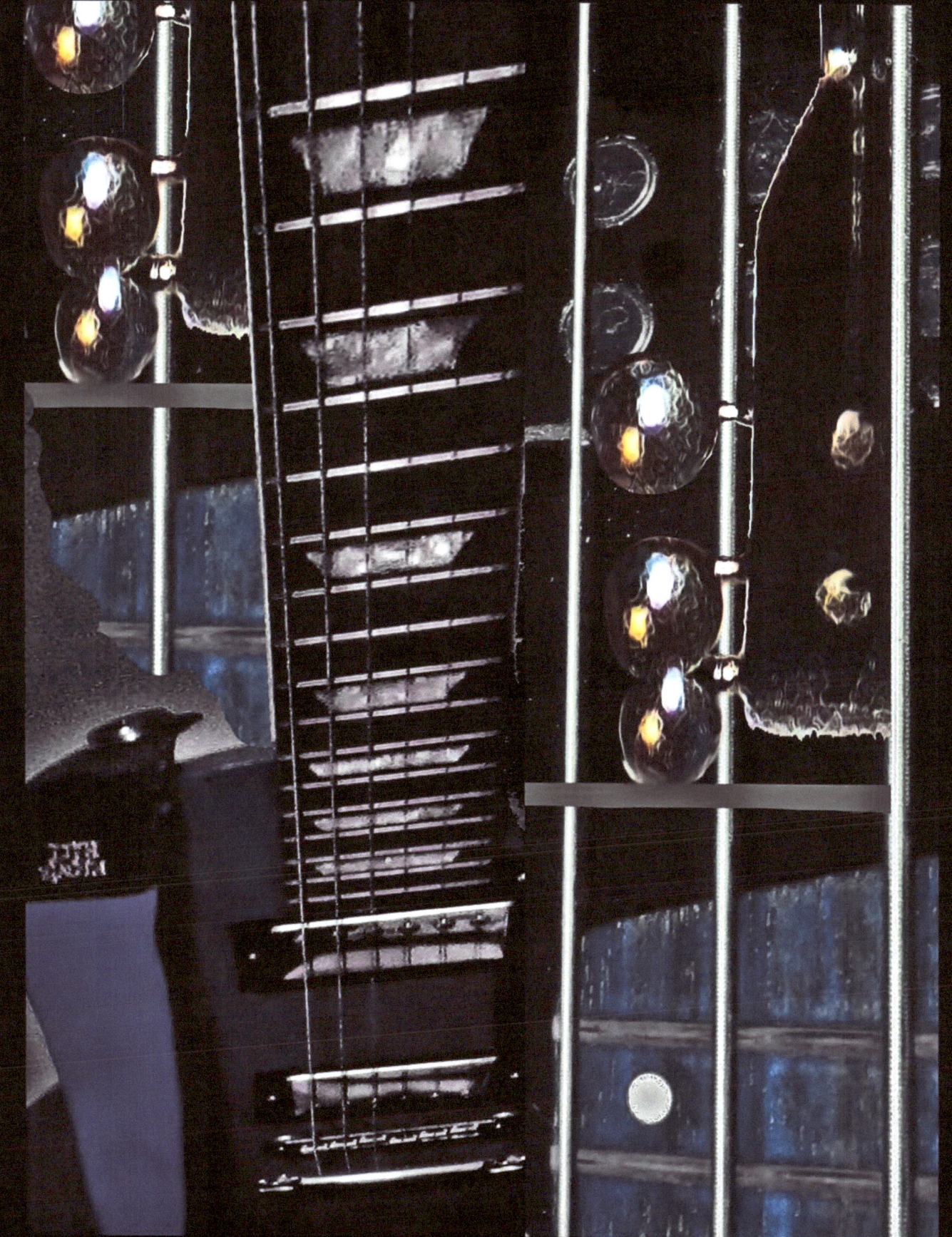

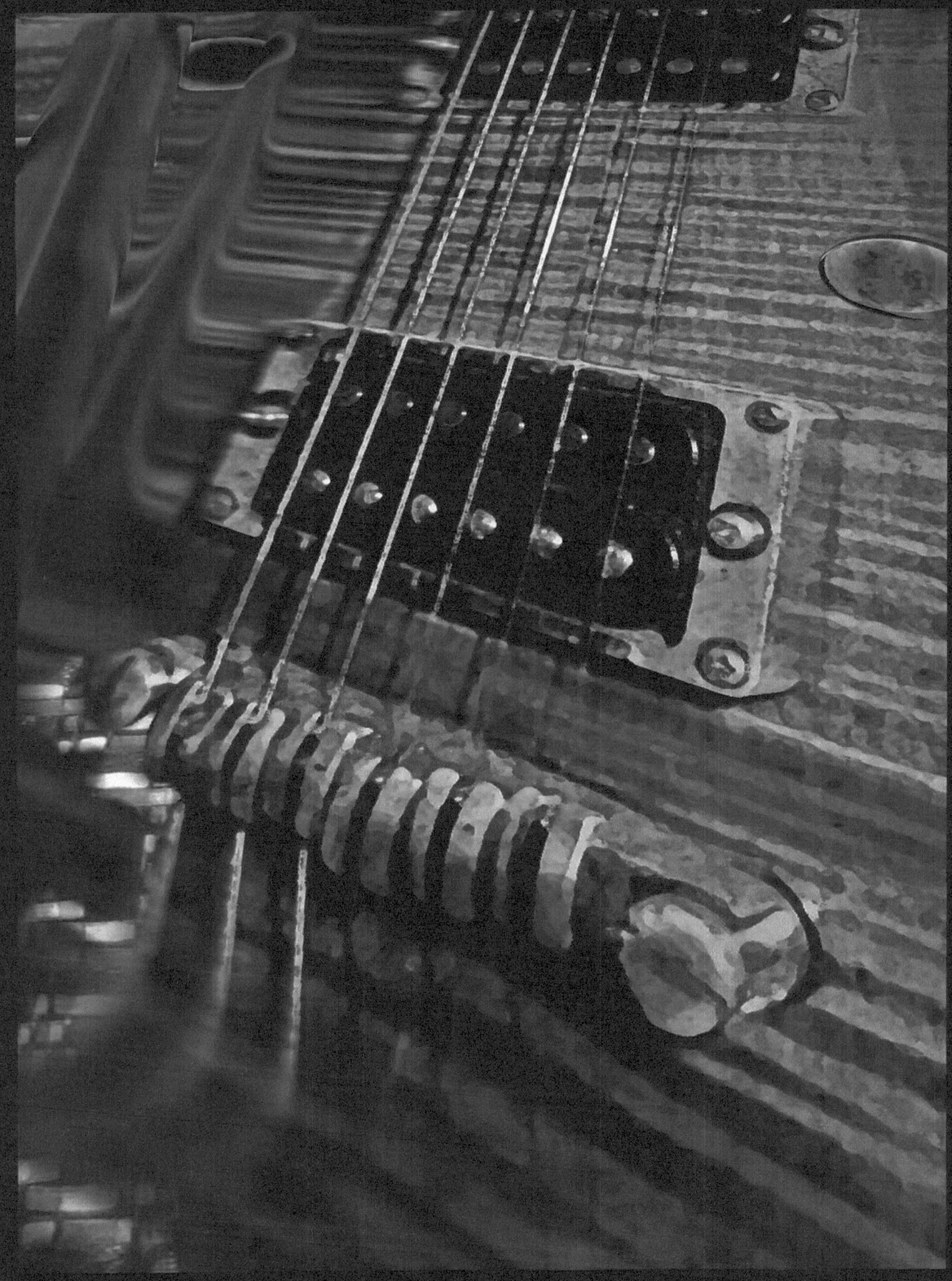

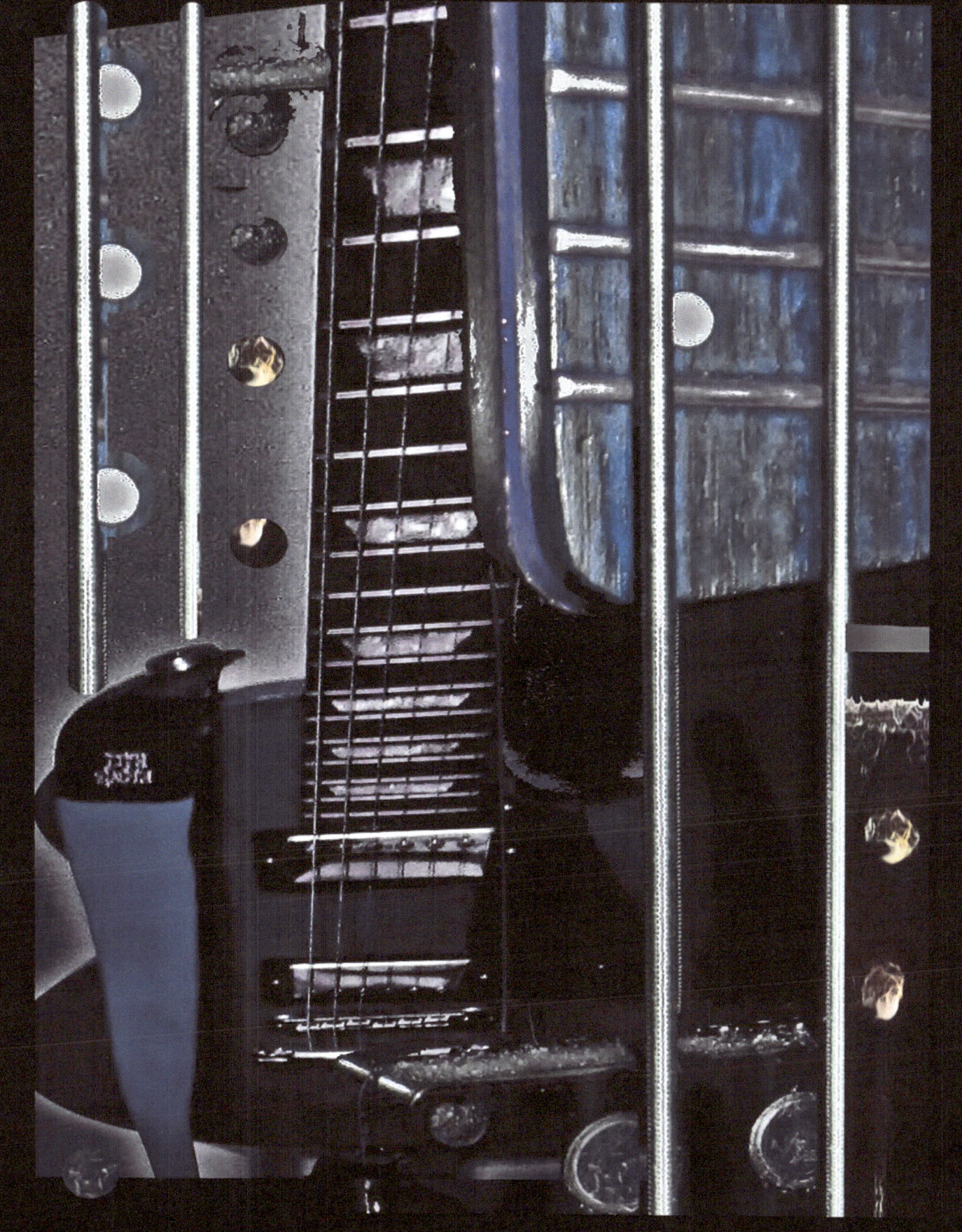

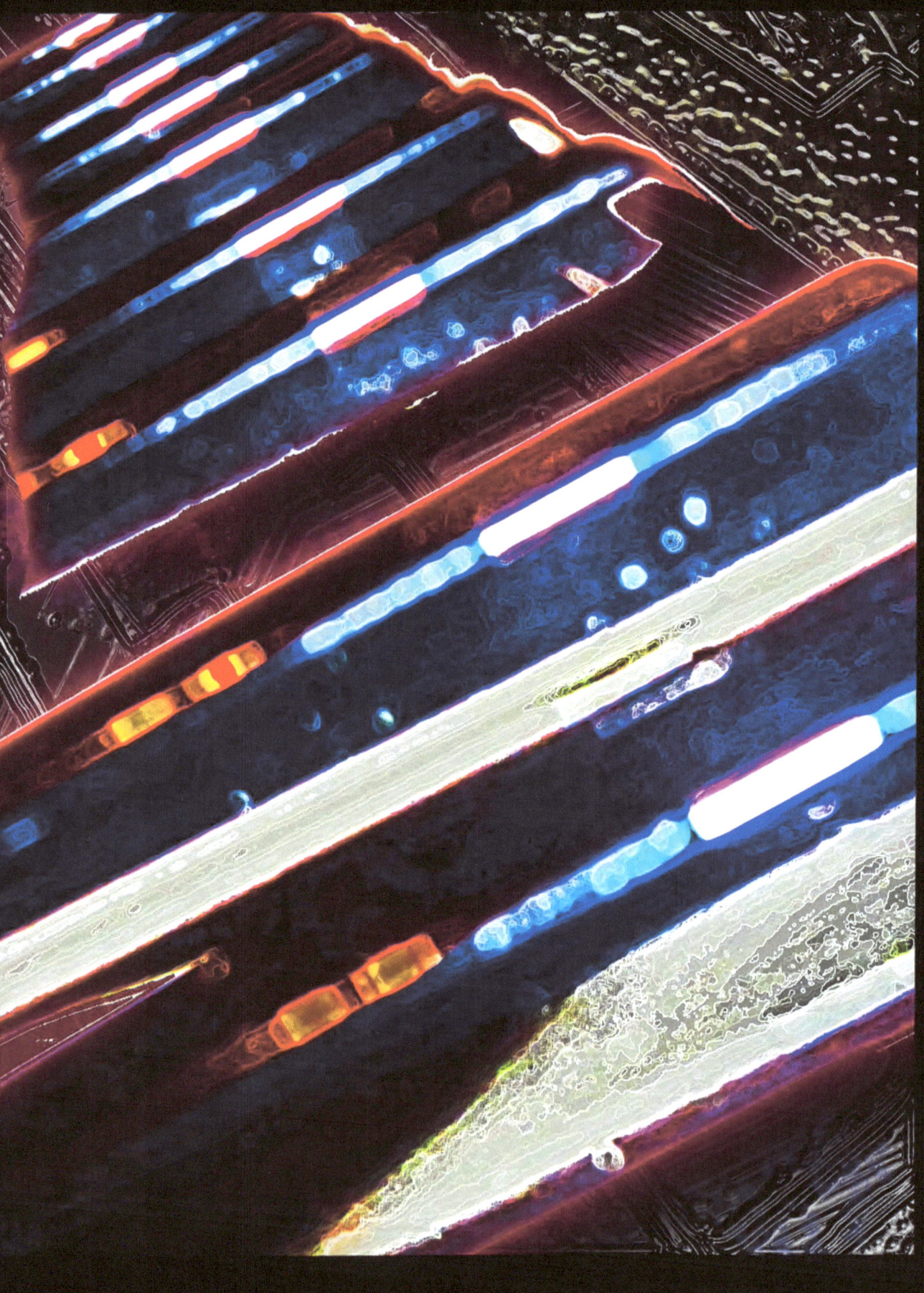

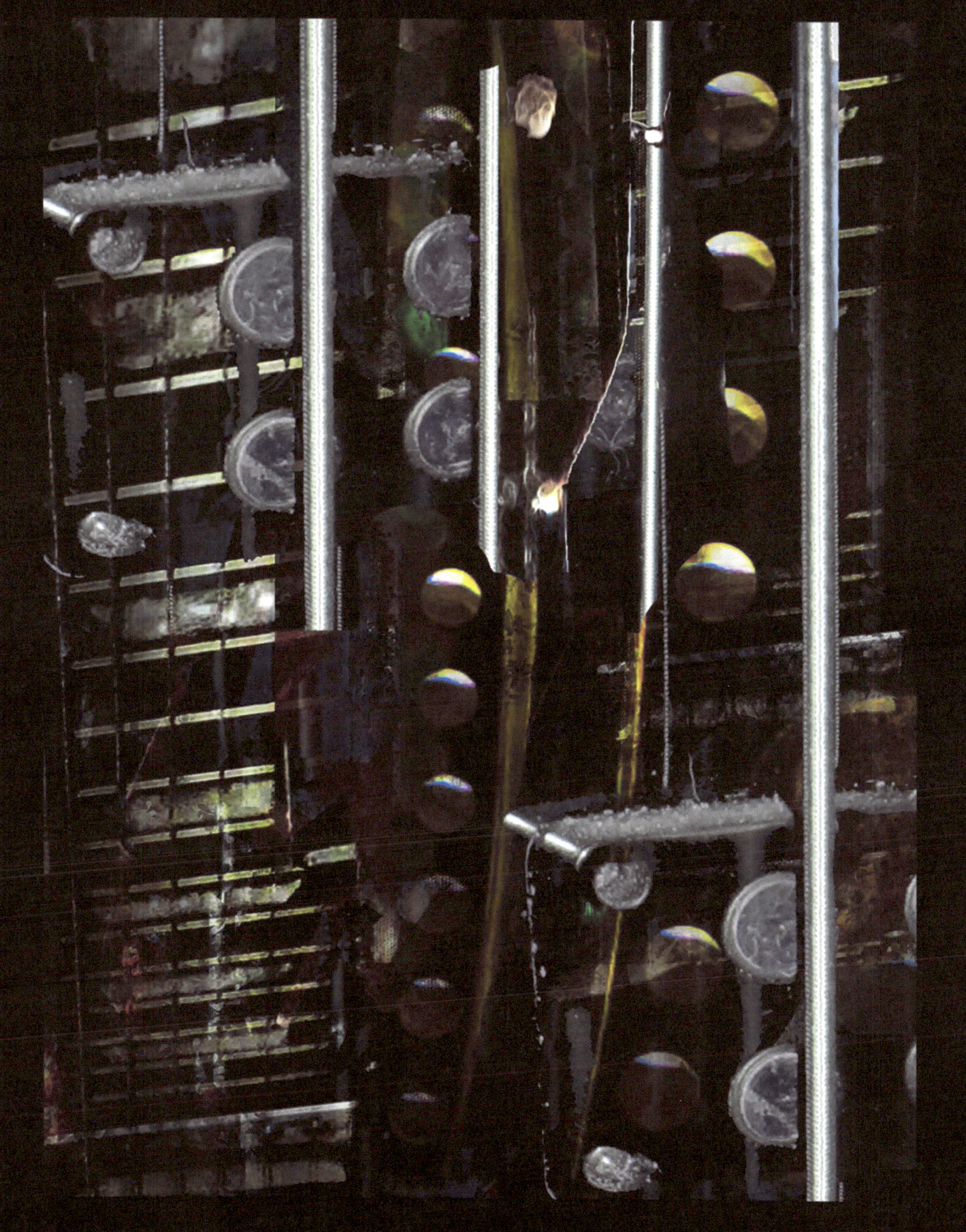

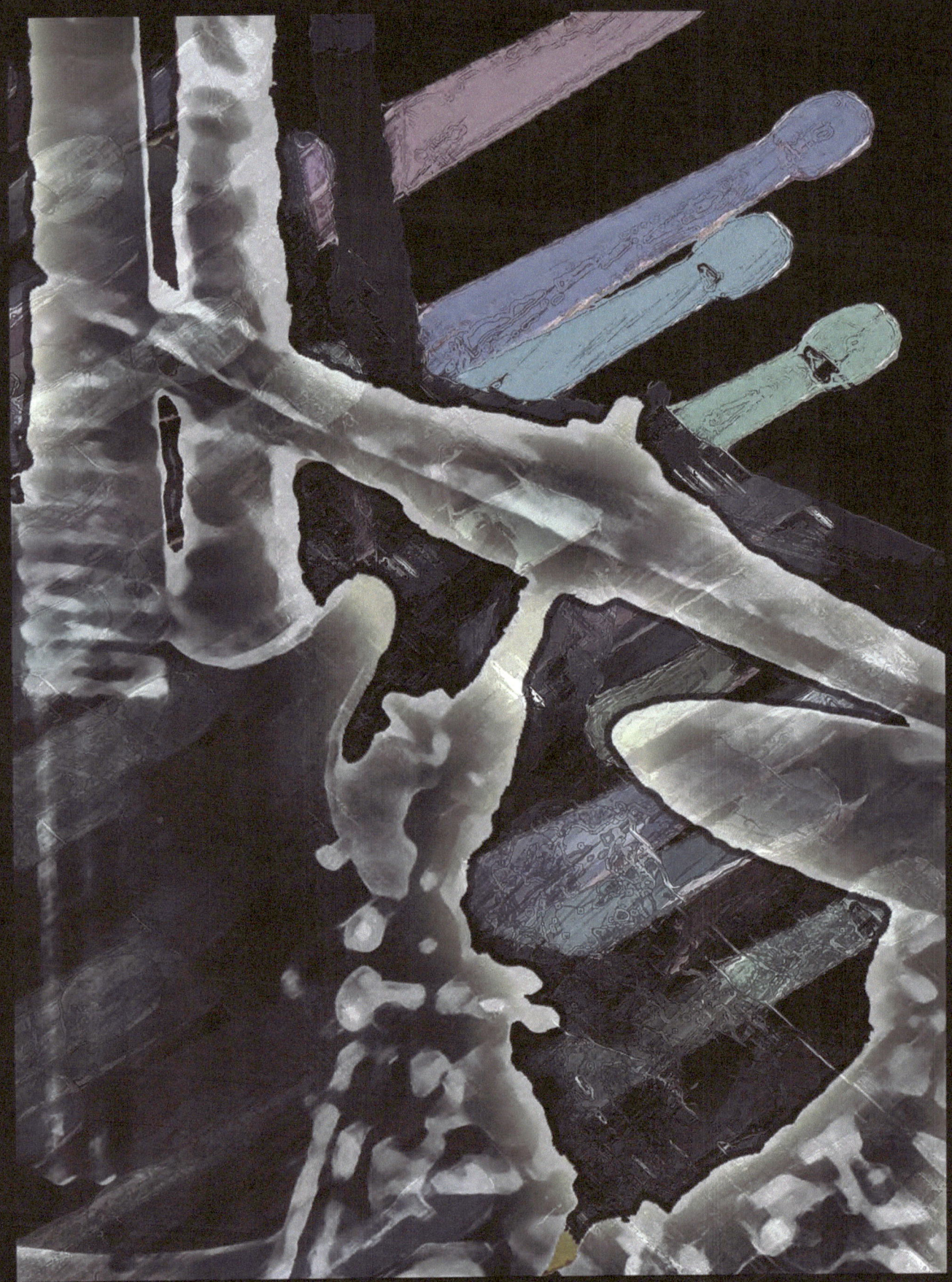

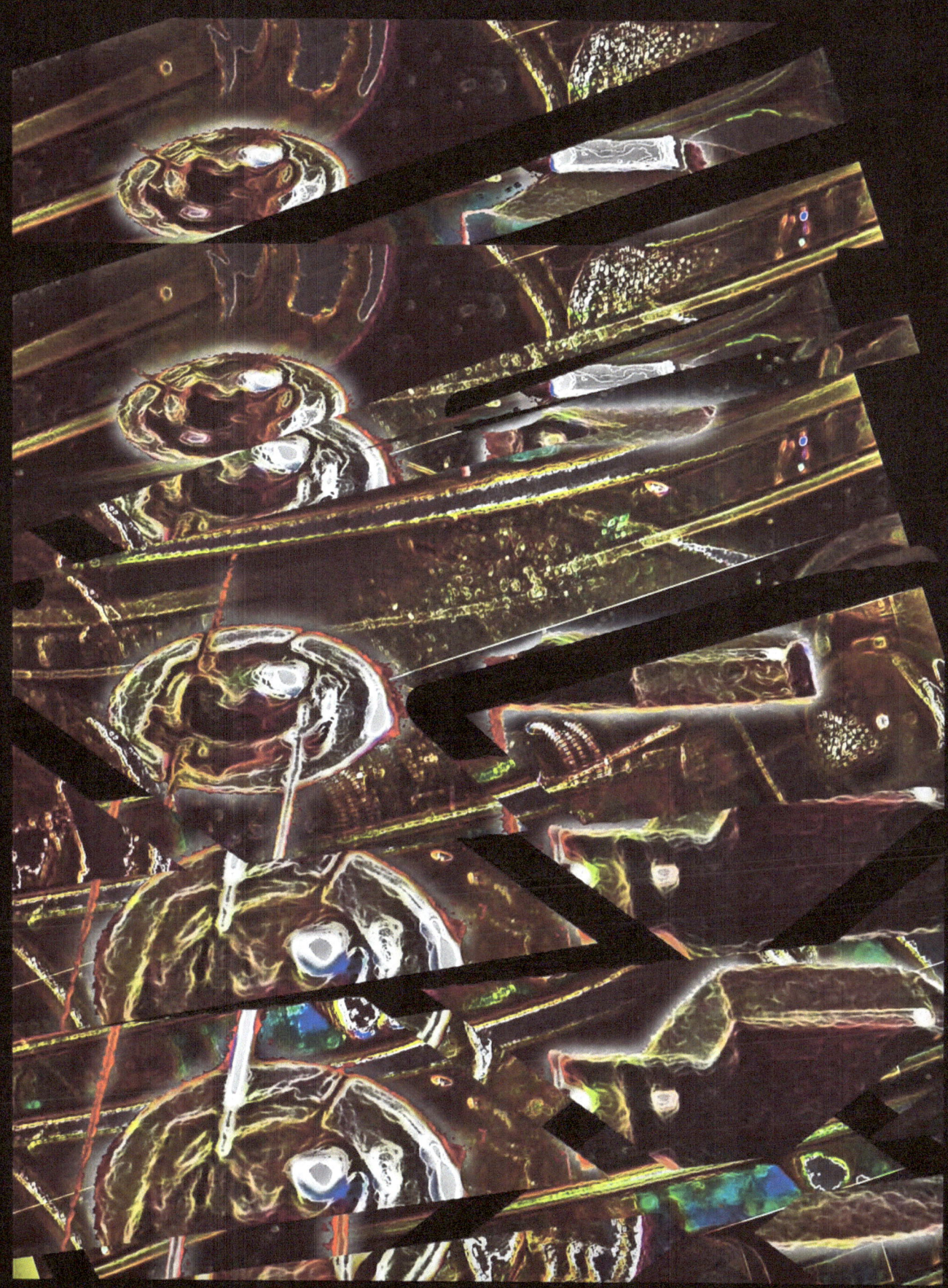

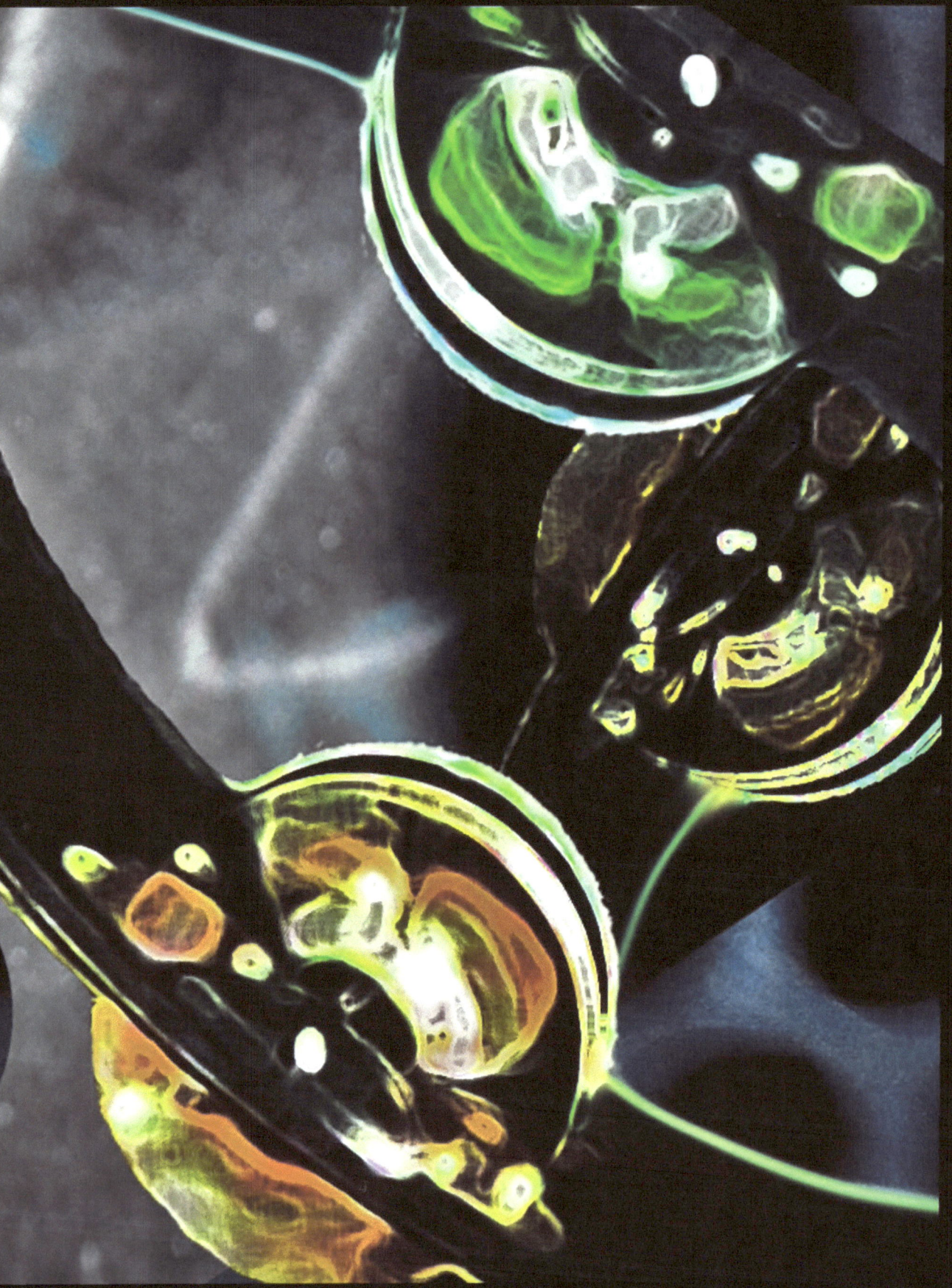

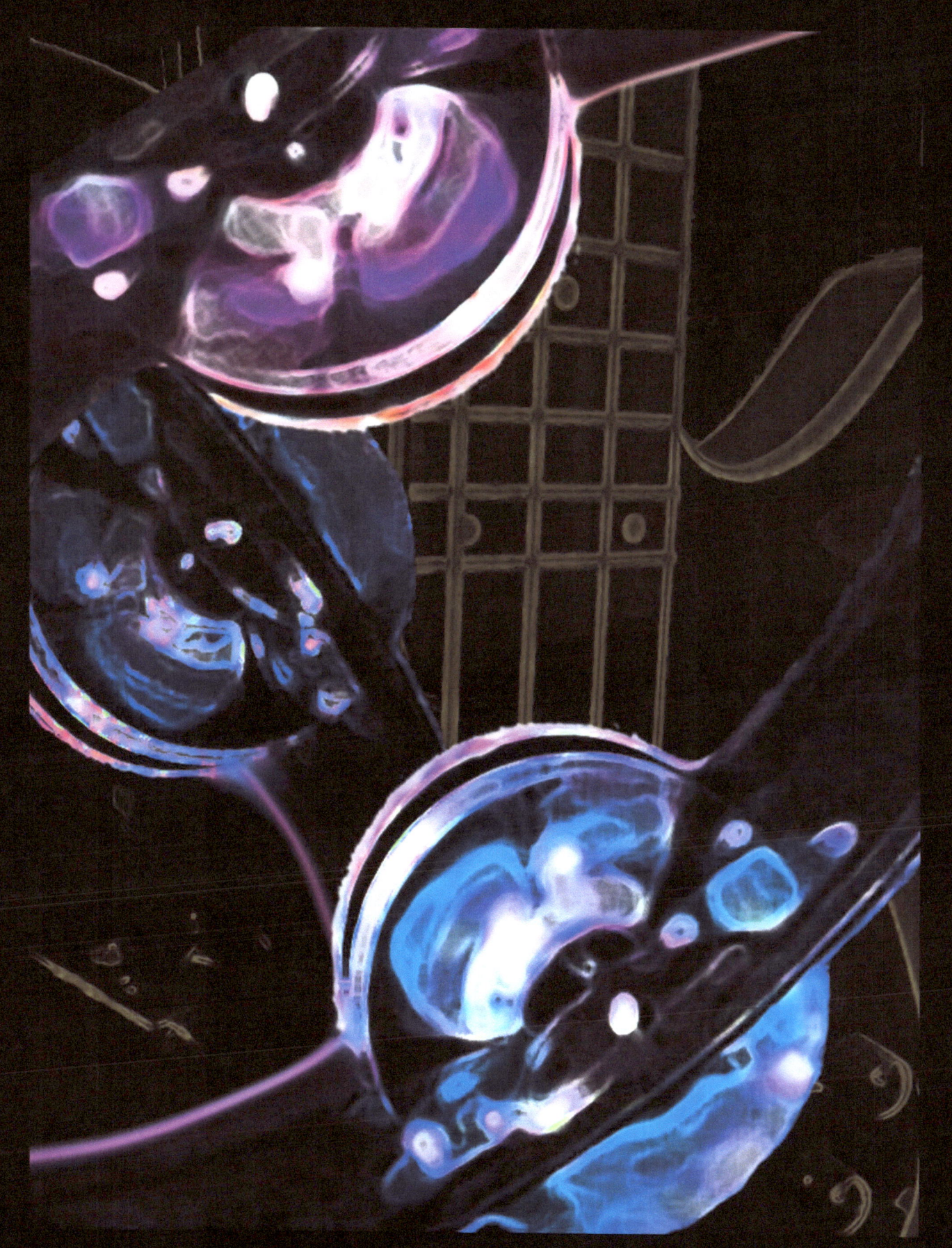

ArtRock

For information on other available graphic books in this series, or to see if your favorite design is available on other items such as wall art, greeting cards or other fun items, email artrock_designs@yahoo.com

All designs copyright R.Geist Designs

www.ingramcontent.com/pod-product-compliance
Lightning Source LLC
Chambersburg PA
CBHW050805180526
45159CB00004B/1551